CHUMS

ALSO BY SIMON KUPER

The Happy Traitor

Football Against the Enemy

Barça

CHUMS

HOW A TINY CASTE OF OXFORD TORIES TOOK OVER THE UK

SIMON KUPER

PROFILE BOOKS

First published in Great Britain in 2022 by
Profile Books Ltd
29 Cloth Fair
London
ECIA 7JQ
www.profilebooks.com

Some of the material in this book originally appeared in a different
form in the *Financial Times* between 2013 and 2021.

'Going, Going' by Philip Larkin (p. 33) from the *High Windows* Collection, with
thanks to Faber and Faber Ltd. 'Autumn Journal' by Louis MacNeice (p. 41, p. 59),
with thanks to Faber and Faber Ltd. Magdalen College Oxford WW1 Memorial
(p. 117), with thanks to The President and Fellows of Magdalen College, Oxford.

3 5 7 9 10 8 6 4 2

Typeset in Dante by MacGuru Ltd
Printed and bound in Great Britain by Clays Ltd, Elcograf S.p.A.

A CIP catalogue record for this book is available from the British Library.

ISBN 978 1 78816 738 3
eISBN 978 1 78283 818 0

FSC
www.fsc.org
MIX
Paper from
responsible sources
FSC® C018072

To understand the man you have to know what was happening in the world when he was twenty.

Attributed to Napoleon (probably apocryphal)

Contents

INTRODUCTION

OXOCRACY

*The keener observers of British public life will have noticed
a particular breed of Establishment men and women.
They're over forty, smugly successful and successfully
smug. Chances are they were also educated at Oxford.*

The Oxford student newspaper *Cherwell*, 24 February 1989

You turn the pages of yellowing student newspapers from the 1980s, and there they are, recognisably the same faces that dominate today's British news: Boris Johnson getting elected president of the Oxford Union debating society; a cheekily grinning Michael Gove among the 'Union hacks in five in a bed romp shocker';[1] and the pair of them being sold alongside Simon Stevens, future chief executive of the NHS, in a 'Union slave auction'.[2]

When I arrived at Oxford aged eighteen in 1988 to study history and German, it was still a very British and quite amateurish university, shot through with sexual harassment, dilettantism and sherry. Gove, Johnson, and the much less prominent David Cameron had graduated just before I arrived, but from my messy desk at the student newspaper *Cherwell*, I covered a new generation of future politicians. You couldn't miss Jacob Rees-Mogg, the only undergraduate who went around in a double-breasted suit, or Dan Hannan, who founded a popular Eurosceptic movement called the Oxford Campaign for an Independent Britain. *Cherwell* was inaccurate, gnomic, a poor imitation of *Private Eye*, badly written in the trademark Oxford tone of relentless irony, with jokes incomprehensible to outsiders, but it turns out with hindsight that we weren't just lampooning inconsequential teenage blowhards. Though we didn't realise it, we were witnessing British power in the making.

I didn't know any of the future powerbrokers personally, because we were separated by the great Oxford class divide: I was middle class, from a London comprehensive (after many years abroad) and they were mostly public schoolboys. I was an outsider who happened to be looking in through the window. Today I am more of an inside-outsider: after a few post-university years living in the UK, I emigrated to Paris in 2002 and have made my life there, but through my column in the *Financial Times*, I have become a kind of corresponding member of the British establishment.

The Oxford Tories – and especially the Etonians among them – were made by many forces besides Oxford. They had been groomed for power since childhood. One classics tutor at Oxford compares Johnson to the ghastly upper-class Athenians in Plato's *Dialogues*: they had been corrupted long before they came to study with Socrates. It's impossible, when discussing the Oxford Tories, to disentangle the overlapping influences of caste, school and university.

But Oxford matters, as an independent variable. Evidence of this is that it's possible to tell the story of British politics in the last twenty-five years almost without reference to any other university. I will argue in this book that if Johnson, Gove, Hannan, Dominic Cummings and Rees-Mogg had received rejection letters from Oxford aged seventeen, we would probably never have had Brexit.

On 24 June 2016, the early morning after the referendum, as I watched the leading Leavers and Remainers traipse across my TV screen, almost all, except Nigel Farage, Oxford types of my generation, I realised: Brexit and today's British ruling class were rooted in the university I had known. Only about 3,000 undergraduates a year attend Oxford, or less than 0.5 per cent of each British age cohort,[3] yet the UK is an Oxocracy. It has been for a while. Of fifteen prime ministers since the war, eleven went to Oxford. (Churchill, James Callaghan and John Major didn't go to university, and Gordon Brown was at Edinburgh.) Three consecutive Oxford Tory prime ministers have ruled the UK since 2010. So how has Oxford captured the British machine? And with what consequences?

In trying to answer those questions, I have always kept in mind that there are many different Oxfords. Lots of students never give a moment's thought to politics. Even among the politically minded, the Oxford of state-school pupils like Harold Wilson, Edward Heath or Margaret Thatcher wasn't the Oxford of Etonians like Harold Macmillan, Cameron or Johnson.

And there are important differences as well as similarities between say, Macmillan and Johnson. The Tory public schoolboy returns in every generation, but each time in altered form. I've tried to understand how the Oxocracy has changed over time, as well as the ways in which it has stayed the same.

A few quick words about what this book is not. It's not my personal revenge on Oxford: I was very happy at university, and learned a fair bit. Having grown up outside Britain, I was enchanted by the banter of Brits who had been trained since infancy to speak well. I also felt blessedly free of the class anxieties that most of the natives seemed to carry around with them. I mooched around Magdalen Deer Park, fell hopelessly in love and made lifelong friendships while playing bad cricket or dissecting indie songs at 5 a.m.

Nor is this book my name-dropping memoir, a jolly boys' story about the japes we all had at university, or my claim to be an outrider of some exclusive power club. It's not an attempt to relitigate the Brexit referendum, or to unearth the many different reasons why 17 million people voted Leave. I'm not suggesting that these people were all manipulated by the Oxford Tories, or by Farage, a major player who barely features in this book. There has been much academic analysis since 2016 of the motives of Leave voters. This book does not enter that debate.

This isn't a twee Oxford tale of witticisms exchanged by long-dead dons. It's not a book about today's somewhat different Oxford. It's not another biography of Boris Johnson.

Rather, it's an attempt to write a group portrait of a set of Tory Brexiteers – overwhelmingly men – from the traditional ruling caste who took an ancient route through Oxford to power. This caste is just a small subset of Oxford.

But it matters because it's omnipresent in modern British political history.

These men were atypical in their beliefs: most Oxford graduates surely voted Remain in 2016. The Tory Brexiteers were a minority even among Oxford politicos in the 1980s. Their fellow students included most of the clique that would surround Cameron's premiership and his Remain campaign, as well as several future senior Labour figures. Johnson and the graduate law student Keir Starmer left Oxford in the same summer of 1987; Cameron graduated a year later.

Much of the media elite of the 2020s was there, too. In 1988/89, two third-year students named Emma Tucker and Zanny Minton Beddoes shared a dingy flat by the canal near the train station. By 2022, Tucker was editing the *Sunday Times*, and Minton Beddoes the *Economist*. The editors of the *Guardian*, the *Telegraph* and the *Daily Mail* in 2022 had also passed through 1980s Oxford. Nick Robinson, presenter of the BBC's *Today* programme, was a Union star of Johnson's era.

But the Tory Brexiteer subgroup dominates this story, because it won. It has ended up making Brexit and remaking the UK. To understand power in today's Britain requires travelling back in time to the streets of Oxford, somewhere between 1983 and 1993.

1

AN ELITE OF SORTS

Oxford is, without a doubt, one of the cities in
the world where least work gets done.

Javier Marías, *All Souls* (1992)

Good A-levels weren't enough. To get into Oxford you
had to succeed in a peculiarly British ritual, the entrance
interview. In 1987, when I went through it, it worked like
this: you are seventeen years old. You are wearing a new
suit. You travel to Oxford. Eventually you find the tutor's
rooms. Perhaps you're served sherry, which you've never
seen before. Then you talk.

The tutors, sprawled on settees, drawl questions about
whatever is keeping them awake. I know an applicant who
was asked, 'Don't you think the Piazzetta San Marco in
Venice looks like a branch of Barclay's bank?' The Oxford
interview tested your ability to speak while uninformed
– to say more than you knew. Many dons of the time
were looking for what they would call 'Renaissance men'
(or even women) who might be fun to teach. They were
free to apply their personal discretion: one tutor I knew
unapologetically favoured tall, blond public school boys

and girls. If you had good school results and could write and talk, you were handed your entry ticket to the British establishment.

Getting in wasn't particularly difficult for white men from the upper middle or upper class – a category that in those days made up the bulk of the intake. Men's colleges had only started to admit women in 1974, to the dismay of many dons,[1] and by the mid 1980s women still only accounted for about 30 per cent of students.[2] (The story told in this book is dominated by men, but that's because the caste I am describing is, too.)

There was little competition for Oxford places from the country's other ranks. In 1980, only 13 per cent of young Britons went into full-time higher education at all.[3] Oxford in 1981 admitted two applicants out of five.[4]

The twenty-year-old Michael Gove summed it up fairly accurately in 1988, when he was president of the Oxford Union: 'Oxford changed only in its admittance of the daughters as well as the sons of the well-heeled middle class.' ('Well-heeled middle class' was a euphemism.) Gove complained that Oxford was 'not truly elitist', meaning not academically excellent.

> It would be a better place if it was ... If we perceived Oxford as the place where our future leaders were educated rather than where our present leaders sent their children to be finished then we might have a healthier society.[5]

Oxbridge in the 1980s still allowed the 'seventh term', the tradition of pupils at private schools staying on after

A-levels for an extra term during which they were coached specifically for Oxbridge entry,[6] complete with practice interviews. When I asked about preparation for the Oxford exam at my comparatively well-favoured comprehensive school, there wasn't any. The head of sixth form told me he didn't want me to go to Oxford anyway, as he didn't believe in selective education.

My school was a former grammar that had gone comprehensive in the early 1980s. The grammars had long been the public schools' main competitors, and their closing by both Labour and Conservative governments (for good and bad reasons) had skewed the field even further in favour of the upper classes.[7] By 1991/92, my last year at Oxford, 49 per cent of incoming students were from British independent schools and just 43 per cent from state schools. (The balance came from overseas.)[8]

If you were from public school and got rejected by Oxford, you might still get in, because it was your school's job to know which tutor to ring to lobby on your behalf. 'One or two telephone calls are still necessary to find places for the borderlines,' noted Westminster's headmaster John Rae in the 1970s.[9] Some lavish dinners for dons may have gone into preparing for those calls.[10]

The future journalist Toby Young, rejected after failing to get the two Bs and a C at A-level that Brasenose College had required of him, was lucky enough to have a father well positioned to phone the admissions tutor himself.[11] Warts and all, Young is a bright man who cannot simply be written off as a member of the undeserving rich. But he got into Oxford only because his father was Michael Young, Baron Young of Dartington, author of the 1945

Labour manifesto, founder of the Open University and inventor of the term 'meritocracy'.

The few outsiders who dared apply to Oxford generally sensed on arrival that they were out of place. A postman's son I know was so scared of meeting people in the days around his entrance interview that, he says, 'I sat in my room in my underpants eating Maltesers'. He ended up becoming an Oxford don himself.

Another Oxford tutor of humble origins recalls, in the 1990s, interviewing state-school kids who would sit perched terrified at the front of their chair. He learned to tell them, 'It's okay, you can relax,' whereupon the pupil would move back two inches. By contrast, one applicant he interviewed – the son and grandson of Oxford men, who had the surname of a past prime minister – leaned back in his chair 'as if he owned the place'. This ex-tutor reports having let in mostly private-school applicants over the years ('we got a bit depressed sometimes'), simply because not many state-school pupils applied.

Fiona Hill, a miner's daughter at a comprehensive school in the north-eastern town of Bishop Auckland, had predictably failed the Oxford entrance exam, which she took without any preparation. The question about Schopenhauer's theory of the will floored her because she didn't know who Schopenhauer was. Hertford, the Oxford college most favourable to state-school pupils, invited her for interview anyway. She arrived there in 1983 in an inappropriate outfit sewn by her mother. While waiting to go into the interview, she spoke to another girl, who, recoiling at her accent, said, 'I'm sorry, but I have no idea what you just said.' When Hill got up to walk into the interview room, a girl tripped her, possibly accidentally, and she fell against a door frame and had to start the interview with a bleeding nose. The kindly don who interviewed her suggested she apply to St Andrews instead. She did, and went there.[12]

Looking back, Hill compared her Oxford experience to 'a scene from *Billy Elliot*: people were making fun of me for my accent and the way I was dressed. It was the most embarrassing, awful experience I had ever had.' She said this in a discussion at a *Guardian* newspaper's members' event, in which she was identified simply as 'Fiona Hill, 50'.[13] By then she had moved to the US, where nobody could place her north-eastern English accent and where she became an academic expert on Russia, a senior White House official, and later a star witness against Donald Trump in his first impeachment trial. Her talents were lost to the UK.

Oxford's detractors and defenders both favour the same term: 'elitist'. But they mean two different things by it. For detractors, 'elitist' refers to the hereditary elite; for defenders, it means the meritocratic elite. In truth, almost everyone who gets into Oxford is a mixture of privilege and merit in varying proportions.

That's true even of Etonians. Eton's mission isn't simply to produce posh gentlemen. It's to produce the ruling class. In the 1920s, an Etonian like Alec Douglas-Home could be admitted to Oxford practically as his birthright, get a third-class degree and still go on to become prime minister, the third consecutive Etonian in the job.[14] From 1900 to 1979, nearly a quarter of all cabinet ministers had been to Eton.[15]

But when the rules changed, and the ruling class

needed to be meritocratic swots who could pass exams, Eton began producing meritocratic swots. Anthony Sampson wrote in his updated *Anatomy of Britain* in 1982 that whereas Etonians had previously been considered 'confident, stupid and out of touch', by the 1980s they were considered 'confident, clever, but still out of touch'. Andrew Adonis explains that Eton was transformed from 'essentially a comprehensive school for the aristocracy ... into an oligarchical grammar school', albeit still filled with mostly 'the same sort of boys'.[16] Their privilege remained intact. Yet by the Thatcher years, many were confident enough to claim that they had risen on merit alone.

Once you arrived at 1980s Oxford, workaholic study was not encouraged. This was an old tradition. Graham Greene reminisced late in life: 'For nearly one term I went to bed drunk every night and began drinking immediately I awoke ... I only had to be sober once a week when I read an essay to my tutor.'[17] Stephen Hawking, who had 'come up' in 1959, found

the prevailing attitude ... very anti-work. You were supposed either to be brilliant without effort or to accept your limitations and get a fourth-class degree. To work hard to get a better class of degree was regarded as the mark of a grey man, the worst epithet in the Oxford vocabulary.[18]

Writing in the 1970s, Jan Morris praised Oxford's fetish of 'effortless superiority': 'The former women's colleges pride themselves on their high proportion of first-class degrees; but their emphasis on brains, on work and on examination results is out of Oxford's character.' Morris complained that 'the new Oxford standards, so ably supported by the women ... prize a first-class mediocrity above an idle genius'.[19]

Ross McInnes, an Australian Frenchman who came to Oxford in the 1970s from a Parisian lycée, and in later life became chairman of the French aerospace group Safran, remarked: 'What struck me about Oxford was the ease with which you could manage academic life and social life and political life. That's very different from France: here, if you go to a [selective] *grande école*, all you do is work, and your academic performance determines the rest of your career.'

In Britain, where university meant living in residence almost unsupervised from the age of eighteen, the principal aim of most students was to have fun and forge lifelong friendships (which would double as career networks). Boris Johnson's page in Eton's Leave Book of 1983 featured a photograph of himself adorned with two scarves and a machine gun, and an inscription pledging to register 'more notches on my phallocratic phallus'.[20]

Safe in the knowledge that you could put Oxford on your CV for ever, you had three years to enjoy this magical place. Most students I knew devoted their energies to trying to grow up, make friends, drink beer, play sport and find love. A survey in my time showed that the average undergraduate worked twenty hours a week during term time – which meant just twenty-four weeks a year. An arts student could get by on four hours' work a week, wrote Allegra Mostyn-Owen, Johnson's college girlfriend and first wife, though she was probably exaggerating for effect.[21]

The American graduate student Rosa Ehrenreich arrived at Oxford from Harvard in 1991. 'The overall ethos of the university,' she wrote later, 'was sufficiently anti-intellectual, laddish, and alcoholic that the best and most interesting undergraduates either voted with their feet by retreating to the privacy of their rooms or, in self-defence, censored their real thoughts and pretended to be as boorish as their peers.'[22] Oxford and Cambridge, she pointed out, had little incentive to raise academic standards because they had a near monopoly on the most highly qualified British students.[23]

Oxford's customer base certainly wasn't very demanding. British undergraduates in the 1980s were studying for free, and had already obtained life membership of the establishment, regardless of how little they actually learned at university. For the rest of their lives they would have a vested interest in perpetuating popular awe of Oxford, so they were unlikely to start doing down the place. Frank Luntz, the American Republican pollster, had a miserable time as a doctoral student at Oxford in the 1980s, but he says: 'When I graduated from there and started to complain about it, I was told by my fellow Oxfordians: "Be quiet. This place is magic, it's going to take you to a lot of places, so don't diss it."'

You were welcome to work hard at Oxford if you wanted. Many students chose to, some to the point of workaholism. But in the 1980s and 1990s, this wasn't obligatory. There were classicists who used their four years at Oxford to read all of Homer and Virgil. Others didn't.

Arts students in the 1980s rarely attended seminars. Lectures were considered an entertainment option, like going to see a film, so only a few famed performers drew an audience. A common student workload was one or perhaps two tutorials a week, for each of which you had to write a shortish essay without footnotes. A common working method was the 'essay crisis': an all-nighter, fuelled by black coffee or 'speed' tablets, followed by a shaky tutorial and then recovery in the college bar.

Essays weren't expected to feature original research. You just had to read bits of a few books, or at least bits of a couple of books (or, if you were really pressed, one book), and then ideally lay out a bold, counterintuitive argument showing that the conventional wisdom about the topic was all wrong.

For your Finals exams, you wrote multiple such papers in three hours while dressed in the dark formal outfit known as 'subfusc'. Men in bowties and women in short black skirts as if they were cocktail waitresses, many tranquillised to the gills, would file into Schools past the university's 'subfusc checkers'.

The provocative essay style tended to come more naturally to men than to women. Elegant writers able to produce in a hurry, and to argue cases they didn't necessarily believe, often did better than serious scholars who had read all the set texts and cared about nuanced complexity. The essay style I absorbed at Oxford turned out to be ideal preparation for a career as a newspaper columnist. Reading the *Economist*, something of a weekly collection of provocative short essays, I see I'm not alone. To my dismay, I recognise a lot of myself in the Oxford Tories: I too learned at Oxford how to write and speak for a living without much knowledge.

Scientists and engineers generally worked harder, with laboratory sessions and essential lectures. But they were a minority: about two-thirds of Oxford undergraduates in the early 1980s studied arts subjects.[24]

At its best, the tutorial system worked beautifully: an hour alone with a brilliant thinker who spent an hour exercising your mind with Socratic questions. One classics tutor at Oxford told me that he saw it as his job to free students from the 'straitjacket' of family and school that had shaped their minds – to help them think for themselves. Sometimes that happened. I still remember the time I was wittering on blithely about Louis XIV imposing some new tax on seventeenth-century France, when the tutor asked, 'So how exactly do you think he did that?' Suddenly I glimpsed the practical issues of trying to govern a territory for most of history. Louis had probably sent out messengers on horseback, and local powerbrokers had either ignored his edict, if it ever reached them, or executed only bits of it.

A clever, self-motivated student could get a lot out of Oxford. A tutor of Ed Balls, the future Labour politician, recalled: 'He understood the subject matter but also thought how you would turn it into policy. One sometimes felt after a tutorial that all your ideas had been sucked out of you. Not only did he want to know about theory X, he also wanted to know what you thought about it and how it could be applied.'[25]

Robin Lane Fox, who tutored Dominic Cummings in ancient history, recalls him as a brilliant, hard-working student fascinated by the great decision-makers from Alexander the Great to Lenin. 'He got a very good First in both parts in three years,' said Lane Fox, adding that Cummings was 'a whole class better intellectually and in Finals' than Johnson. Cummings did not spend his Oxford years polishing his rhetoric. 'I'm not articulate,' he has claimed, in what seems to be a jibe at his political peers with their 'moronic' debates.[26]

But academically speaking, most of us got rather less out of Oxford. When I reread my essays while revising for Finals, they were so pathetic that I felt like writing to my tutors to apologise. Very often a tutorial would go like this: aged eighteen, hungover and distracted by a thousand other things, you'd read out your pitiful but elegant essay, which you'd finished at 5 a.m. The tutor would point out the gaps in your knowledge. For an hour, you'd try to talk your way around those gaps.

One tutor pointed out a flaw in my argument by quoting something that the French thinker Roland Barthes had said about reality being a construct. I replied, 'Barthes thought reality was a construct, but then he was run over by a laundry van,' which was about the only thing I knew about him. I thought I'd made a hilarious joke. 'He was,' agreed the tutor, and he allowed me to move on. He was a fellow at another college to which I'd been farmed out, and improving my mind wasn't his priority. It wasn't mine either.

Bluffing your way through tutorials was considered an art. *Cherwell* once praised Simon Stevens (who went on to run the NHS from 2013 to 2021) as 'Oxford's most talented off-the-cuff tutorial faker': 'Recently Simes read out almost half of an essay to his tutor before his partner revealed that he was "reading" from a blank piece of paper.'[27]

Of course, tutors generally knew what tutorial fakers were up to, but as one tutor later told me: 'You can tell whether a student is bluffing. The question is whether you can be bothered. Tutors have seen so many people like you. There's just a bulk of really rather dull students who are quite forgettable.'

If a student wanted to waste his three years drinking beer, many tutors in the 1980s felt that that was his affair. Younger tutors tended to be more invested in their own research. Some older tutors had got their jobs in bygone amateur days, didn't have PhDs, might make it to retirement without ever publishing an academic paper, and lived off sherry. Alcohol – abundant and free at High Table – was an institutionalised element of the Oxbridge don's life in the 1980s. Margaret Grieco, of the Institute of Transport Studies, said that in her husband's first three months as fellow of a Cambridge college at the time, he went from being a 'very moderate drinker' to existing in an almost continuous drunken state.[28]

In short, a lot of 1980s tutors couldn't care less if the student hadn't written the essay or was talking without knowledge. And in any case, as I have since discovered, talking without knowledge is useful preparation for professional life – more useful than, say, an understanding of Roland Barthes. You could leave Oxford in my day transformed by the world's best staff-to-student ratio, or having learned nothing except how to bluff your way in a plausible accent. Even Roy Jenkins, the university's chancellor from 1987 to 2003, admitted that Oxford at its worst was 'glib and flippant'.[29]

Kalypso Nicolaïdis, Oxford professor of international

relations, now on leave at the European University Institute in Florence, says:

> If a student is capable of producing two well-written essays a week, with well-structured arguments, they can kind of get away with not knowing much about the subjects. This may sound superficial, but communicating is useful in life. Sometimes you need to convince people succinctly, especially if you go into politics. Oxford will reward it.

But, she adds,

> [I]t's not what Oxford is about. Why would I want to be a professor at this university if this is what it's about? If you ask the faculty, we would say, 'No, our dream and our commitment is to convey knowledge as deeply as possible.' Whether as a student you want to take advantage of this is up to you.

One-on-one tutorials allowed dons great discretion, especially those who taught in the 'college rooms' where they lived. A tutor at my college was known for exposing himself to students, and also for trying to recruit some of them into the intelligence services. Like most things in 1980s Oxford, his habits were treated as a bit of a laugh. Another don I knew was such a serial harasser of his female tutees that finally the college cracked down: he was banned from tutoring women one-on-one.

Political correctness was not rampant at the time. In 1985, most colleges had either one or zero female fellows.[30]

A female contemporary of mine who studied philosophy, politics and economics (PPE) emailed me: 'We didn't study a single twentieth-century philosopher, not a single woman anywhere in sight – in the set texts, on the teaching staff or mentioned in any way at all the course of three years of study of humanities!' She recalls one tutor lamenting to her and her tutorial partner that they weren't little boys. She says: 'I think the point was to unnerve us and intimidate us – and it did.'

The colleges in the 1980s could still appear like 'men's clubs with ladies' wings'.[31] In my time, some male undergraduates who had sexually assaulted a woman in their college's 'Front Quad' were eventually suspended, for one term. At meetings of my college's junior common room, if a woman tried to speak, it was customary for men to chant: 'Get your tits out for the lads!' A Sikh student elicited the cry (which nobody challenged): 'They're letting in towelheads now!' Homophobia was taken for granted. Any complaints about these traditions were treated as evidence of humourlessness.

2

CLASS WAR

Public schoolboys go forth into a world that is not entirely
composed of public school men, or even of Anglo-Saxons,
but of men who are as various as the sands of the sea; into a
world of whose richness and subtlety they have no conception.

E. M. Forster, 'Notes on the English Character'[1]

The working class was represented at the university chiefly by the college servants, who ranged from porters to 'scouts' (essentially, cleaning ladies). Some of them worked for the same college from their teens until their pensions. Their West Country accents were often mocked, sometimes lovingly. In the 1980s, the Oxford they came from was in free fall. In 1936, Cowley, a suburb down the road from the colleges, had had the biggest car factories in the world outside the US.[2] But during the 1980s, this dominance was collapsing. Oxford's car-making workforce shrank from about 25,000 in the 1970s to 5,000 by the early 1990s.[3] True, the car jobs were replaced by new ones in the city's burgeoning service sector, but these didn't necessarily go to the same people. In the square mile of undergraduate Oxford, the carnage was a faint offstage rumble.

Among the largely southern English student body, entire categories of the British population were scarcely represented. The only Afro-Caribbean student at my college wrote an undergraduate thesis on Afro-Caribbeans at Oxford. I remember asking him, 'What's the percentage of Afro-Caribbeans at Oxford?' He said, 'Percentage? There are six Afro-Caribbean undergraduates in the whole university.'

The essential class structure of undergraduate Oxford was bipartite: middle classes versus upper classes. Toby Young captured this in a chapter in a 1988 book called *The Oxford Myth*, a collection of essays by recent undergraduates, edited by Boris Johnson's sister Rachel. In what would become his trademark style of deliberate offensiveness, Young divided undergraduates into two categories: 'socialites' (by which he meant the upper classes) and 'stains', the 'small, vaguely deformed' breed, with acne and anoraks, who hadn't been to posh schools, who came 'from areas like Slough, Bracknell and Milton Keynes' and who 'would scuttle across quads as if they had mobile homes on their backs'.[4]

I had spent most of my childhood outside England, and was shocked by the country's tradition of schooling each class and gender separately. Most middle-class undergraduates had come from comfortable state schools (often the few surviving grammars), or from private day schools. Nevertheless, within the Oxford context these people could congratulate themselves on their bootstrap origins. Here is Young's modest reply to the question of whether he was a member of the posh Bullingdon Club: 'No. I'm a comprehensive boy; the Buller wasn't for the likes of me.'[5]

(In fact, he and I attended the same school on the edge of Hampstead Heath.) Similarly, when Dominic Raab ran for Tory leader in 2019, the one thing that distinguished him in a field consisting almost entirely of Oxford males was that he had been to state school: a grammar in leafy Buckinghamshire. In one interview, he boasted of not having had a nanny ('No!').[6] Even Dominic Cummings (Durham School) could protest on Twitter on behalf of two fellow private schoolboys: 'If u think me Gove & Boris are posh you have literally no idea what posh is.'[7] That was setting the bar for poshness rather high.

Oxford's upper-class sheen could be intimidating to middle-class and the small cohort of working-class students. In the 1980s, 'the place felt like one huge public school to which a few others of us had been smuggled in by mistake,' recalls Andrew Adonis.[8] Many outsiders arrived at Oxford uncertain, terribly dressed and trying to find themselves. Suddenly they had to stride into dining halls wearing gowns, and stand for graces in Latin. Some (especially women) wrestled with imposter syndrome, convinced they had been wrongly admitted, fearing, as the working-class boy Dennis Potter had in the 1950s, that Oxford 'would be full of intellectual giants'. ('It was full of sick pygmies,' he concluded.)[9]

One tutor told me in 2019 that female or less posh students often needed constant reassurance that they were clever enough to be at Oxford. By contrast, students from what he called the 'Jacob Rees-Mogg brigade' needed constantly to be told that they weren't as clever as they thought.

Middle-class students needn't have been so worried.

The British establishment is perennially on the lookout for fast-rising outsiders to recruit to the ranks. One function of Oxford has always been to select these people and initiate them into ruling-class life, complete with servants. Whereas on the continent the rising middle classes largely displaced or beheaded the aristocracy, in Britain they 'could themselves acquire some of the attitudes, and speech inflexions, of the upper class by having the education of "gentlemen"', writes A. N. Wilson in *The Victorians*. The system expanded the British elite's talent base, and neutered potential revolutionary leaders.[10]

And so, during their time at Oxford, new recruits were trained to feel at ease in establishment settings. One contemporary of mine, the lower-middle-class son of a single mother, found himself facing an age-old dilemma at a formal dinner early in his time at university: which of the many forks and knives by his plate was he meant to use? To his relief, the presiding don announced: 'For those who are not used to this amount of cutlery, you start at the outside and work in.' At the same dinner this man received another piece of advice that has guided him through a successful establishment career: 'When there's a fruit course, never eat the orange, because it squirts.' Going through Oxbridge for people like this, writes Walter Ellis, 'is the second baptism. Your parents are forgiven you; go and sin no more.'[11] But the upwardly mobile often paid a price: permanent separation from their parents, home town and childhood friends.

Public schoolboys tended to find Oxford underwhelming, a step on their path that they'd seen coming since early childhood. I call them 'public schoolboys' partly because school for them was a more formative experience than for the rest of us. Boarding schools in particular helped create a toff caste, into which selected outsiders like Johnson – a child of the bohemian upper middle class – could be initiated by learning the codes and speech rules from age seven. 'The [boarding-school] experience was designed to produce a shared mindset,' wrote Richard Beard in *Sad Little Men*.[12]

While we had spent eight hours a day with our classmates, the public schoolboys had spent twenty-four. We had been shaped chiefly by our parental homes, whereas they had been defined by school, which often branded them with nicknames that effectively replaced their given names. In Johnson's case it was the reverse: the uninitiated knew him by his nickname, Boris, but only intimates called him by his real name, Al. The delineating effect was the same: one name for insiders, another for outsiders; upstairs, downstairs.

For toffs who had been to a particularly 'hereditary' school like Eton, their connections with their schoolmates' families might go back generations. For an Etonian like Cameron, school would always remain his tightest network: it was Eton more than Oxford that would provide him with some of his closest aides and political allies, notably his chief of staff, Ed Llewellyn, his minister for government policy, Oliver Letwin, and the chair of the Number Ten Policy Board, Boris Johnson's brother, Jo. My argument that Oxford is an independent variable shaping British power applies more to Johnson, Gove, Hannan et al. than it does to Cameron.

Most public schoolboys grew up almost entirely within

their caste. Stanley Johnson, Boris's father, claimed to have never met a grammar-school boy before Oxford.[13] Boris Johnson himself described the caste members as 'a loosely knit confederation of middle-class undergraduates, invariably public-school, who share the same accents and snobberies, and who meet each other at the same parties'. (Note, again, that deceptive term 'middle-class'.) These people had 'an English middle-class distaste for political conversation', wrote Johnson, and yet they made a natural political machine.[14]

I have since read that some upper-class students mocked the middle classes as 'grockles' or 'plebs' as well as 'stains'. I don't remember ever hearing those terms at Oxford, perhaps because I didn't spend enough time with toffs. Only one per cent of the British population attends boarding schools,[15] but so many from this caste went to Oxford that they were able to separate themselves into their own private universe. Boarders like Johnson arrived at university already knowing dozens of people from school. Once at Oxford, their class networks were automatically activated, and they met the toffs they didn't yet know. This meant that they didn't particularly need the rest of the student population, except for attractive women. (There was a chronic shortage of women among the Oxford toff classes, because fewer female toffs were put on an Oxbridge track.)

Rees-Mogg told me,

The benefit of Eton on going to Oxford is that you are used to some of the things that Oxford has. You are used to living away from home, and a lot of your contemporaries aren't. I think that is an advantage. I had been used to being educated in beautiful old buildings, I had grown up with that, that was very much part of my life. That helps with the Oxford experience.

In the 1980s, the upper classes were regaining the confidence that had been beaten out of them during Britain's social democratic 1945 to 1979 era. In that period the UK had lost its superpower status, and had been overtaken economically by much of western Europe, but on the other hand, more than ever before, it had become One Nation. In 1979, British 'income inequalities reached their lowest point ever recorded', writes Danny Dorling, professor of geography at Oxford.[16] But then along came Margaret Thatcher, who restored inequality.

Though she saw herself as a scourge of ossified castes, she was a proud defender of wealth and private schools. During her reign, privilege and the right accent became something to be celebrated again. At Oxford, fading dining societies were revived. Dafydd Jones, a young local photographer who began photographing Oxford undergraduate parties in the early 1980s (and was still photographing some of the same people as London powerbrokers decades later), recalled in 2020:

... the students were no longer dressing like long-haired tramps. Suddenly formal dress and black tie were becoming de rigueur. I saw this partly as a fashion reaction to the dressing-down style of the Sixties and Seventies. With hindsight, it was after the election of Margaret Thatcher, and the rich were benefitting from generous tax cuts and had started to feel confident again.[17]

In 1981 Granada Television screened Evelyn Waugh's *Brideshead Revisited*. The hero, the teddy-bear-wielding Oxford undergraduate Sebastian Flyte, is a dissolute Etonian with floppy blond hair and languid charm. The TV series (rather than Waugh's novel itself) helped shape the atmosphere of 1980s Oxford. It created an aura of camp glamour around the toff as throwback.

Waugh's imagined 1920s Oxford may never quite have existed, yet it was strangely recognisable to the wealthier students of the 1980s. The intervening six decades had brought Depression, war and social democracy. Now, for the first time since the original *Brideshead* generation, a cohort of Britain's gilded rich could enjoy Oxford without worrying much about either boring left-wing ideologies or the wider world. The 1980s were the age of the roaring Sloane in a dinner jacket, proud to offend unemployed 'townies'.

Around the time of *Brideshead*'s screening, the *Sunday Times* journalist Ian Jack visited Oxford to write a feature about the new generation of students. An undergraduate named Rupert Soames, Churchill's grandson, told him, 'You see, students went through the 60s thinking the world was organised in a bad way and that they could do something about it. Absolutely wrongly, as it turned out. Now people take themselves less seriously, which is very, very attractive.'[18]

Soames explained,

We're a group of people who've come up to Oxford with a base of friends from school, and on the whole we're richer than the average student and we tend to have famous parents.

The fancy-dress part is simply to turn the party into an event; you either make people drive a long way to your place in Northumberland or you make them dress up. So we give parties a theme, and in Oxford these themes can be disgusting at times.

'Such as?' asked Jack.

'Clitoris allsorts,' said Soames.

Soames told Jack his ambition: 'To be rich and to love and marry a beautiful woman.' Jack asked how rich. 'Very, very rich. As rich as one can possibly be.'

Even people who didn't belong to Soames's 'group of people' wanted to join in the fun. The future right-wing journalist James Delingpole, a relatively ordinary middle-class boy from Birmingham who at Oxford dressed up like a Tory squire, would recall, with a laugh: 'I wanted to be adopted by the aristocracy.'[19] Owen Matthews, today a writer on Russia, says:

The appeal was primarily aesthetic. Consciously or unconsciously, we copied Waugh's strange mixture of adoration and irony. I thought it was beautiful to smoke oval cigarettes and hang out with girls in floaty dresses. We spent a lot of time in black tie throwing each other in the pond. I thought it was the spirit of the place. In our brogues and tweeds, eating straw-berries in punts, we were playing at being members of this lost world, and the star player was Jacob Rees-Mogg. It just seemed an antidote to the decline and lack of aesthetics which we'd known in our child-hoods. I remember growing up in the 1970s eating dinner by candlelight with rubbish out on the streets.

But most public schoolboys of the 1980s differed from Waugh's feckless Sebastian Flyte in one decisive respect. They wanted to 'get on', to become rich and famous in Thatcher's Britain. They had arrived at Oxford already equipped with a ruling-class accent, rhetorical skills and the ability to feel confident in any establishment setting – qualities that the rest of us picked up only at university. Boys from schools like Eton or Winchester came from families that expected success, and that put no ceiling on ambition.

Crucially, too, whereas most children are raised in homes where they are loved unconditionally, boarders grow up in institutions where they are valued for their looks and achievements. Success became the cloak that they wore in life. Boris Johnson's chapter titled 'Politics' in his sister's book wasn't about ideals. It was about how to hack one's way to the political zenith.[20] Looking back at Oxford, he would reflect: 'What a sharp-elbowed, thrusting and basically repellent lot we were … When Toby Young began an article in *Cherwell* with the words, "I work harder and achieve more than anyone else I know", we all chortled in approval of this ghastly ethic.'[21]

I got a peek into the upper-class world at the end of my first year, when an Oxford friend invited me to the open day at his old boarding school. It was one of several voyages of discovery that I made to the homes of university friends around Britain, from Hampshire through Stockport to Northumberland.

This time, after a train journey deep into the southern English countryside, we had dinner in my friend's old 'house' at school. The housemaster and his wife knew my friend well, and were eager to hear how he was getting on at Oxford. We slept in a dormitory room with about ten other boys, and were woken at 7 a.m. by a bell. I felt sorry for them. In my childhood I had had a private space, a bedroom of my own, a home where I could escape the pressures of adolescent public life.

I spent much of the open day standing on the boundary watching the cricket match between the school and the Old Boys, dumbstruck with admiration. These were boys of about my age, cricket-mad like me, but their technique was classes better than mine. The pitch was perfect, and beside the field were the nets where they had been schooled day in, day out, by professional coaches.

At tea, the headmaster gave a talk to the parents in which he gloated about Labour's defeat in the 1987 general election, more than two years earlier. He took it for granted that Labour, which had hoped to take the public schools down a peg, was regarded by everyone present as the enemy, an evil force intent on destroying the world that he and the parents treasured. The headmaster's underlying message was that the privilege that his boys had had thrust on them aged seven or eleven was right and normal and time-honoured, and that only 'socialists' could dream up anything so unnatural as taking it away. I sensed that I was in the presence of a caste. Here was the class solidarity that

Marxists talked about, but in the upper class rather than the proletariat.

*

One sensation from that visit that stays with me more than thirty years later is the aesthetic pleasure. My friend's school, perched in its rural splendour, could have been a film set for Brideshead. Growing up in this sort of idyllic English setting shaped the public schoolboys. When not away at school, many had lived in an idyllic rural family home, generally in southern England. The country they loved was ancient and unspoiled, or at least had been crafted by the Victorians to look ancient and unspoiled.

Ancient, unspoiled English beauty was more than their aesthetic. It was their ideology, the core of their world-view. The hero of *Brideshead Revisited* isn't actually Sebastian Flyte; it's an ancient English country house, Brideshead itself, always under existential threat from modernity.

For Waugh, Brideshead was the soul of England, even if only a tiny fraction of the English population lived in anything like it. Ancient English buildings might even be the point of the whole national enterprise. Boris Johnson in his days as *Telegraph* columnist defended 'sickeningly rich people' on the grounds that 'if British history had not allowed outrageous financial rewards for a few top people, there would be no Chatsworth, no Longleat'.[22]

Architecture is the most tangible element of the heritage that separated the toffs from everyone else. As one childhood friend of Cameron's remarked: 'He is a real, proper Englishman, who would love to defend what he sees as the real England, but his real England is different to almost everyone else's.'[23]

When Oxford Tory nostalgics glimpsed the outskirts of Oxford itself – the sort of ugly post-war landscape where most Britons lived – it tended to strike them as a horrendous aberration. Oxford's 'factories and the housing estates feel like intruders upon some ancient preserve',[24] wrote Jan Morris. The city had become 'an unplanned model Motopolis', grumbled John Betjeman, who thought 'the approaches to Oxford are the worst thing about it'.[25] The Oxford don J. R. Tolkien based 'The Shire', paradisical home of his hobbit creatures, on the lost West Midlands village where he had grown up before it was swallowed by the Birmingham suburbs.[26]

Kingsley Amis complained in 'Their Oxford':

To reach the centre you turn left, not right,
And drive halfway to Abingdon before
You start to double back past building-site,
Paella joint, hair-stylist, hi-fi store,

By uncouth alleys to the old hotel,
Now newly faced ...[27]

Amis's Oxford friend Philip Larkin cast these accusations against the entire nation:

And that will be England gone,
The shadows, the meadows, the lanes,
The guildhalls, the carved choirs.
There'll be books; it will linger on

In galleries; but all that remains
For us will be concrete and tyres.[28]

And Roger Scruton wrote in his 'funeral oration' for England: 'The old England for which our parents fought has been reduced to isolated pockets between the motorways.'[29] After Scruton's death in 2020, Johnson tweeted from Downing Street: 'We have lost the greatest modern conservative thinker.'[30]

Conservatives like Scruton, Johnson and Cameron located the 'real England' in the pre-industrial past. They found another version of it in the square mile of central Oxford. This fraction of the city where most students lived appeared untouched by anything since the Civil War. Oxford had 'never been bombed or burnt', noted Jan Morris.[31] Its preservation wasn't entirely accidental: British powerbrokers had a sentimental attachment to their former playground. In 1956, a longstanding plan to build a road through Christ Church Meadow actually reached Britain's Conservative cabinet. Peter Snow writes: 'At the height of the Suez Crisis [the cabinet] found time to debate the matter and, not unexpectedly (five of its members were Christ Church men) stalled the proposal.'[32] The road was never built. Today, Christ Church remains such a perfect specimen of unspoiled ancient England that it could serve as a set for the Harry Potter films.

Standing in a college quadrangle at night, you couldn't always tell by looking around whether the year was 1988 or 1688. The university felt sixty miles and several centuries removed from London. Timelessness had its intellectual upsides. At Oxford, it was possible to treat the present as a fleeting moment that shouldn't obscure the past millennia. At best, that attitude could encourage a life of the mind free of contemporary concerns or fads. A tutorial about John Stuart Mill was entirely about Mill, and not an argument about Thatcher.

On the other hand, there were downsides to living in the past. 'Oxford is very pretty, but I don't like to be dead,' said T. S. Eliot.[33] Anthony Sampson, author of *The Anatomy of Britain*, thought 'the spells and enchantments' of Oxford and Cambridge encouraged their graduates 'to be preoccupied with the past, to assume that structures are permanent and unchanging'.[34] The timeless paradise of Oxford inspired its inhabitants to produce timeless fantasies like *Alice in Wonderland*, *The Hobbit*, *Narnia*, and, incubating from the late 1980s, Brexit.

3

A LITTLE LEARNING

Yes, I could have been a judge but I never had the Latin.
I never had the Latin for the judging. I didn't have
sufficient to get through the rigorous judging exams ...
And so I managed to become a miner – a coal miner. I
managed to get through the mining exams – they're not
very rigorous. They only ask you one question. They
say, 'Who are you?' And I got 75 per cent on that.

Peter Cook, playing a miner in the early 1960s
comedy revue *Beyond The Fringe*[1]

You can read the fault lines of today's British elite in the
subjects that they studied at Oxford. Maths and sciences
in Britain had long been marked (to use Nancy Mitford's
terminology) as 'non-U': something that toffs didn't do.
George Orwell wrote of his prep school: 'Science was not
taught in any form – indeed it was so despised that even an
interest in natural history was discouraged.'[2]

This attitude prevailed even in the cases that seem to
offer the most obvious counterexamples. Charles Darwin,
who went to Shrewsbury School, wrote, 'Nothing could
have been worse for the development of my mind than

Dr Butler's school, as it was strictly classical, nothing else being taught except a little ancient geography and history.' Darwin complained that his master 'rebuked' him for showing interest in the natural world.[3] In the early 1860s, just after *Origin of Species* was published, the headmaster of Shrewsbury told the Clarendon Commission on public schools: 'The natural sciences do not furnish a basis for education.' Most MPs who debated the matter in parliament agreed.[4]

Alan Turing was pushed towards classics at Sherborne, his headmaster writing to his parents: 'If he is to be solely a *Scientific Specialist*, he is wasting his time at a public school.'[5] Stephen Hawking studied physics at Oxford because his college didn't offer maths.[6] In 1980s Oxford, science students were mocked as 'Northern Chemists'[7] – a trope of Rachel Johnson's book. Allegra Mostyn-Owen, in her essay on drugs, included a carefully worked put-down: 'Nigel estimated that about thirty per cent of the people he knew at Oxford, i.e. the visible sort – not the scientists – dabbled in any kind of dope.'[8] There are echoes here of Charles Ryder in *Brideshead* dismissing his upstairs neighbour as 'a mouse of a man connected with the Natural Sciences'.[9]

Britain does have world-class scientists, engineers and quants, but they are stuck in the engine room while the rhetoricians drive the train. Modern Oxford has specialised in producing the politicians and civil servants who administrate the British state, the lawyers and accountants who service the economy, and the pundits who narrate the show. These people (and I'm one of them) typically dropped science and maths at school aged sixteen, and acquired only a smattering of economics. In parliament in 2016, MPs who had studied politics at university outnumbered those who had studied engineering nearly sevenfold.[10]

Numbers have historically been a challenge for Britain's ruling class. Douglas-Home as prime minister admitted to using matchsticks to work out the consequences of the Budget.[11] Later British leaders struggled to judge scientific advice on nuclear energy, climate change and Covid-19. In 2010, George Osborne became chancellor with no formal post-school education in economics or business beyond whatever he had picked up in his Oxford history degree. By the late 2010s, Oxford's most oversubscribed under-graduate degree was economics and management,[12] but during Osborne's student days it didn't yet exist.

Oxford's dominant technocratic degree at the time was PPE: philosophy, politics, economics. Any three-year undergraduate degree is only going to skate the surface, but that was triply true of PPE, which spread the student's time across three subjects (although most people dropped one after the first year). A PPEist of my day told me, 'I went on to work in the Treasury but could never use the economics part of my degree as it wasn't good enough.'

Since the referendum of 2016, it has become commonplace to associate Brexit with PPE. Ivan Rogers, for instance, a grammar-school boy who read history at Oxford, and the UK's permanent representative to the EU until he resigned in 2017, discerned in Brexit 'a very British establishment sort of revolution. No plan and little planning, oodles of PPE tutorial level plausible bullshit, supreme self confidence that we understand others' real interests better than they do ...' But this is a misdiagnosis.

In fact, in the 2016 referendum, 95 per cent of MPs who had studied PPE voted Remain.[13] They included Cameron, Jeremy Hunt, Philip Hammond, William Hague, Matt Hancock, Liz Truss, Rory Stewart, Sam Gyimah, Damian Hinds, Nick Boles, the Milibands, Ed Balls, Yvette Cooper and Peter Mandelson. Most of these people were modernisers at heart, who had presumably chosen the degree in search of the cutting-edge knowledge needed to run a serious country. Among the rare PPEists to back Leave were Rishi Sunak, and, more consequentially, Rupert Murdoch, who in 1950s Oxford had been business manager of *Cherwell*. (Murdoch had also stood for secretary of the Labour Club,[14] but was disbarred from holding office after an investigation into electoral malpractice conducted by the young Gerald Kaufman.)[15]

By contrast, all the leading Oxford Tory Brexiteers studied backward-looking subjects: classics for Johnson, history for Rees-Mogg and Hannan, and ancient and modern history for Cummings. Gove's degree was English, which mostly meant the canon.

The most Brexity degree among MPs in 2016 was classics: six of the eight classicists in the Commons voted Leave.[16] Classics was a particularly public-school course, because so few state schools offered Latin and Greek. Rachel Johnson, who read classics at Oxford one year below her brother Boris, recites a few lines of Latin, then reflects: 'All these things we had to learn by rote, so they stuck in the head, and you got into Oxford.'[17] By the time their brother Leo arrived, there were three Johnson siblings reading classics at Oxford simultaneously. Their brother Jo arrived in 1991 but did history.

In those days, if you came from the right class, classics was the easiest mainstream degree to get in for: in 1981, two years before Boris Johnson started his degree, Oxford admitted three-quarters of pupils who applied to study classics.[18] Yet perversely, classics carried outsized prestige. Such was the status of Latin that it had been part of the admissions requirement for Oxford and Cambridge until 1960.[19] Francis Crick, who could never be bothered to learn the language, failed his entry exams for both universities. He went to University College London instead,[20] before co-discovering the structure of DNA.

In the gentlemanly Oxbridge tradition, the less useful your degree, the more chic it was. As the poet Louis Mac-Neice noted,

> Not everyone here having had
> The privilege of learning a language
> That is incontrovertibly dead.[21]

Precisely because Latin and Greek were taught chiefly at public schools, both languages became ruling-class markers – as Johnson knows when he recites from the *Iliad* in public. (While mayor of London, he enlisted his former Oxford tutor Jasper Griffin to provide classical passages for his speeches.)[22] Rees-Mogg later said he regretted not having studied classics at university: 'All the really clever people do that.'[23]

'The classics fulfilled the same sociological function in Victorian England as calligraphy in ancient China – a device to regulate and limit entry into a governing elite', explained the historian Colin Shrosbree.[24]

Happily, there aren't many canonical Greek and Latin texts, and somebody like Johnson who had been studying the languages since prep school had read the main ones years before Oxford – a competitive advantage over fellow classicists who had begun learning Greek and Latin only for A-levels, or even at university. In his second year he dropped ancient history, the part of the classics syllabus that happened to require the most hours in the library.

His tutor in classics, Jonathan Barnes, recalled, 'If you're intelligent enough, you can rub along in philosophy on a couple of hours a week. Boris rubbed along on no hours a week, and it wasn't quite good enough.' When Barnes told him off for copying a translation straight out of a textbook, Johnson reputedly apologised: 'I've been so busy I just didn't have time to put in the mistakes.'[25] As Waugh remarked in *Brideshead*: 'Those that have charm don't really need brains.'[26] Johnson did have brains, but he had discovered at school that he had too much charm to bother using them to the full. He treated his degree as nearly four years of leisurely revision, followed by what Anthony Kenny, Master of Johnson's college Balliol, described as 'six weeks of really hard work' before Finals.[27] Because Johnson was a skilled essayist, that was almost but not quite enough to get him his First. Rachel recalls that it later fell to her to 'break the terrible news' to him that their brother Jo had got his.

*

The dominant personality in the history faculty in 1980s Oxford was Norman Stone. His reputation as an unabashed groper[28] didn't stop him being appointed to the university chair in 1985. Stone was a fantastically entertaining lecturer: at 9 a.m., gripping his lectern in both hands to stop himself falling over from drink, he could ad lib about European history in a Glaswegian accent, without notes, non-stop for an hour. He found Oxford small-minded, bureaucratic, liberal, even 'Marxist': 'I hated the place from the moment that I arrived ... To adopt the words of the gospel according to St Matthew, "It had been better had these people not existed" ... I've never been in a more absurd place.'[29]

His intellectual approach, recalls an Oxford colleague of his, was 'you see a consensus and you run towards it and headbutt it'. Stone was one of Thatcher's few apostles at the university, and occasionally acted as her adviser. With his instinct for breaking things, he despised Tory Wets and what he saw as soft-right weaklings like John Major. He called students 'smelly and inattentive',[30] yet was easy for undergraduates to get to know, usually in the pub, though I remember encountering him at a drunken student party. As a politically incorrect, hellraising, Thatcherite early Eurosceptic, he exercised a fatal attraction for historically minded young Tories. Dominic Cummings reportedly approached him after a lecture to complain that his own tutor was always telling him to ignore the role of individual decision-makers like Hitler. Stone agreed that this was insane, and said, 'Boy, I'll teach you myself,' which he did. The two men developed a mutual fascination.

Another of Stone's protégés, Hannan, would write of his memorial service in 2019:

I was able to take my place in St Martin-in-the-Fields

among hundreds of (for want of a better shorthand) conservative intellectuals. There were dozens of Tory peers and MPs, scores of distinguished writers and academics and a good number of those anti-communist Mittel-European thinkers who, in many ways, made up Norman's hinterland.

Arriving just in time from the European Parliament, I found myself between Peter Lilley and Alan Sked, the LSE historian who founded the Anti-Federalist League in 1991, changing its name to UKIP in 1993. Dominic Cummings ambled in a little late wearing what looked like a black gilet for the occasion. Michael Gove and Andrew Roberts were among those who gave readings. You get the picture: here was the tribe massing to mourn one of its own.[31]

But Stone's focus on Europe was unusual in 1980s Oxford. The undergraduate history degree was heavy on what was called 'English' (not British) history. 'It was Anglocentric and it was constitutional,' recalls a historian of Britain who has tutored at Oxford for thirty years. The syllabus was then still recognisably descended from the one that William Stubbs, the future Bishop of Oxford, had drawn up in the 1870s. The compulsory modules English I, II and III took the student from Roman Britain to modern times. At the heart of the degree was parliament, and the Reform Acts by which the ruling classes had, gradually and wisely, extended the franchise to the lower orders. The syllabus consigned the entire rest of the world to 'general history'.

'There was a sense that you were enschooled in a narrative of the English past,' says the veteran tutor. 'The very structure of it was high-political. At the centre of this world-view, which stretches to Madras and Melbourne, is Westminster.'

Most people who had studied history at Oxford – like most Oxford graduates full stop – almost certainly voted Remain in 2016. But public schoolboys came to the history degree from a very particular starting point. The Anglo-centric, Westminster-centric degree felt personal to them. This wasn't simply the history of England. It was the history of the ruling class, and therefore their family history. Nowadays women and ethnic minorities often complain that nobody in their schoolbooks looks like them. For the public schoolboys, it was the opposite: almost everyone in their schoolbooks looked like them. Rees-Mogg recalls studying prime ministers such as Walpole, Peel and Palmerston (all of them Eton or Harrow and Oxbridge). He told me: 'I didn't sit there thinking, "Gosh, this will be me in a few years' time". But I certainly thought that a political career was going to be a potentially interesting thing to do.'

Boys like him absorbed not so much the Great Man as the Great Toff view of history. The message of their books: a few brilliant, white British public schoolboys could overcome tedious practical obstacles and dominate the world as long as they were willing to scrap for it.

The British ruling caste was a warrior caste, which had left ancestors on countless foreign fields. For the public schoolboys, the Second World War was just one more episode of the glorious British past, not the heart of the story as it was for most of the population. A panoply of wars occupied places of honour in the toffs' history books.

Charles Ryder in *Brideshead* contrasts himself with his fellow officer Hooper, a non-martial, lower-middle-class youth from the Midlands:

> Hooper was no romantic ... The history they had taught him had had few battles in it, but, instead, a profusion of detail about humane legislation and recent industrial change. Gallipoli, Balaclava, Quebec, Lepanto, Bannockburn, Roncevales, and Marathon – these, and the Battle of the West where Arthur fell, and a hundred such names whose trumpet-notes, even now in my sere and lawless state, called to me irresistibly across the intervening years with all the clarity and strength of my boyhood, sounded in vain to Hooper.[32]

The history of Empire, too, was personal to the toffs. After all, the public schools and Oxbridge had educated the men who, in the Catholic writer Ronald Knox's phrase, 'when they've finished playing here ... can go out like good little boys and govern the Empire'.[33] Ten out of twenty viceroys of India went to Oxford,[34] as did Cecil Rhodes, who called the university 'the energising source of Empire'.[35]

In public-school history classes in the 1970s and 1980s, Empire was often presented as a manly romp. James Wood, the *New Yorker*'s literary critic, recalls of his time at Eton, where he was a contemporary of Johnson and Cameron:

> First-year boys were taught by generalist teachers, usually classicists, who instructed us in English, Latin and history. For history, we were given *Heaven's Command*, the first volume of Jan Morris's trilogy

about the rise and fall of the British Empire, along with extracts from the other two volumes.

The trilogy is a lush, romantic account of the enormous, bloody, dust-filled adventure of empire. Morris – who as James Morris had fought in the 9th Queen's Royal Lancers during the Second World War – describes military expeditions, noble defeats and brutal victories with the same rousing relish. It was a good book to give to dreaming 13-year-old boys.

Wood quotes the closing set piece of Morris's trilogy, Churchill's funeral in London in 1965. 'For the last time the world watched a British imperial spectacle,' she wrote. 'A hundred nations were represented there, and twenty of them had once been ruled from this very capital.' Wood comments:

I read those words when I was 13 and have never forgotten them: propaganda has such supple power. What a sentence. And what an idea! History ended in 1965. I read those words, and so did David Cameron, and so – I'm sure – did Jacob Rees-Mogg, who triples down on this sickly imperial nostalgia in his recent book [*The Victorians: Twelve Titans Who Forged Britain*], telling us in his acknowledgments, amid nods towards patient wife and beneficent nanny, that 'it was *Heaven's Command* by Jan Morris that sparked my interest in history'

If you were the adolescent Rees-Mogg or Boris Johnson, these stories of Great Toffs were intoxicating. The boys would carry this version of history in their heads for ever. Wood says Rees-Mogg's *The Victorians* 'reads like a collection of recycled Eton essays originally done in detention as punishment', and notes that Johnson's hagiography of Churchill 'effectively ends' with a Morrisian account of that 1965 funeral.[36]

Perhaps no other country has as happy a relationship with its own history. And the self-appointed guardian of this relationship is the Conservative Party. The Tory public schoolboys grew up as ancestor-worshippers, and understandably so: for anyone able to gloss over the brutality of Empire, the achievements of their tiny caste were breathtaking. Between about 1860 and 1960, British men who had attended either independent schools or Oxbridge or both had invented, ruled and written much of the modern world. They had governed a quarter of the planet, and overseen victory in two world wars. They created Alice in Wonderland, Peter Pan, Sherlock Holmes, Winnie-the-Pooh, Bertie Wooster, James Bond, *The Jungle Book* and *Nineteen Eighty-Four*. They had spilt the atom and discovered evolution, television, penicillin and the structure of DNA. They helped invent the computer and the nuclear bomb.[37] They gave the world Keynesianism and most modern sports. Recall Boris Johnson's camp British-exceptionalist speech as mayor of London at the end of the Beijing Olympics:

> Virtually every single one of our international sports were either invented or codified by the British, and I say this respectfully to our Chinese hosts who have excelled so magnificently at ping pong. Ping pong

was invented on the dining tables of England in the nineteenth century and it was called wiff waff. There I think you have the essential difference between us and the rest of world. Other nations, the French, looked at a dining table and saw an opportunity to have dinner. We looked at a dining table and saw an opportunity to play wiff waff.[38]

And the list of this caste's achievements could be extended endlessly. I once found myself up a mountain in the Alps writing about a group of British toffs who went skiing every winter in 1920s outfits. As I scribbled in my notebook, a female toff peered over my shoulder and drawled, 'Oh, are you writing shorthand? My great-great-grandfather invented shorthand.' 'What was your great-great-grandfather called?' I asked. 'Pitman,' she said. I was writing Pitman shorthand.

After all that, if you were born into the ruling caste in the 1960s or 1970s, modernity could only feel like decline. Your fathers and grandfathers had run the world, and here you were, growing up in a struggling mid-sized outpost of the European Economic Community. The UK's tame, vegetarian, low-stakes, Brussels-based, post-imperial incarnation had nothing more glorious to offer than the Falklands War. The American pollster Frank Luntz, who was at Oxford from 1984 to 1987, told me in 2021: 'What America's going through right now is what the UK was going through when I was there: "We've peaked".'

Johnson's generation felt the shame of late birth. Luntz's fellow American Rosa Ehrenreich diagnosed in early 1990s Oxford:

They were born to a poor island, still rigidly conscious of the glorious past, and told to adjust to the unglorious present and the gray future represented by Prime Minister John Major.

No wonder they sulk! No wonder work hardly seems worth the effort … No wonder they try to recreate the certainties of the past, with dining societies, rugby, the academic traditions of the Victorians.[39]

Many 1980s public schoolboys transmuted these feelings into a camp nostalgia for greatness. When Johnson as foreign secretary visited the golden pagoda in Yangon, Myanmar, he began reciting Kipling's poem 'Mandalay': 'Come you back, you British soldier.' The British ambassador had to warn him quietly that this was 'not appropriate'.[40]

4

BULLER RULES

*There is tradition behind the Bollinger; it numbers reigning
kings among its past members. At the last dinner, three years
ago, a fox had been brought in in a cage and stoned to death
with champagne bottles. What an evening that had been!*

Evelyn Waugh, *Decline and Fall* (1928)

The most famous photograph of 1980s Oxford, probably
taken in 1987, is a group portrait of 'Dave' Cameron, Boris
Johnson and eight other young men on the steps of Tom
Quad in Christ Church College, wearing the tailcoats, blue
bow ties and mustard-coloured waistcoats of the Bullingdon
dining club. Toby Young calls it their 'ruling-class uniform'.

None of the ten is smiling; someone presumably told
them not to. An outsider, remarked Rachel Johnson, would
see in the picture 'a group of upper-class public schoolboys ... who know in their heart of hearts that they'll
be running the country in twenty-five years' time'.[1] The
picture became so notorious an image of an entitled ruling
class that the photographers, Gillman and Soame, eventually withdrew permissions to publish it.[2] Labour had
reportedly been planning to use it as a campaign poster.[3]

Other Bullingdon alumni include George Osborne, Johnson's brother Jo[4] and the sometime Polish foreign minister Radek Sikorski. Rory Stewart claims to have attended one dinner before deciding it wasn't for him.[5] In fact, it's such an exclusive public schoolboy club that I'd never heard of it until years after leaving Oxford. I probably didn't even know anyone whom the Buller would have bothered rejecting for membership. (Yet the club wasn't exclusive enough for some: Charles Spencer, Johnson's close schoolfriend and brother of Princess Diana, was elected a member but declined to join.)[6]

The Bullingdon was defiantly anti-meritocratic: almost all its members were selected on the basis of their social origins and gender. It specialised in public statements of entitlement. Club members went around in a pack sacking restaurants or the rooms of new members, smashing bottles on the street,[7] humiliating hired sex workers, and 'debagging' (removing the trousers of) lower-caste outsiders. They would then add insult to injury by compensating 'pleb' victims with money. The message: *The rules don't apply to our class.* After all, Bullingdon members were the people who were going to make the rules. That's why Eton is more lenient about rule-breaking than are less prestigious public schools. To cite just one example: whereas schools in the 1980s often expelled pupils for smoking pot, Eton merely 'gated' fifteen-year-old David Cameron for about a week.[8]

One night in 1987, several Bullingdon members were arrested after somebody threw a pot plant through a restaurant window. Johnson later claimed, 'The party ended up with a number of us crawling on all fours through the hedges of the Botanical Gardens, and trying to escape police dogs. And once we were in the cells, we became pathetic namby-pambies.'[9] One club member who was arrested said later that Johnson's claims to have been held overnight at Cowley police station were untruthful boasts. The same man identifies the only three members who escaped arrest that night: Johnson, Cameron (who had run off down a side street), and their fellow Old Etonian Sebastian Grigg, now the fourth Baron Altrincham. Even at the height of a drunken night, this trio was able to think of their CVs. A decade later, all three stood as candidates for parliament in the 1997 general election. The anonymous club member told the *FT* in 2010: 'Maybe we always thought we were going to be running the country. Certainly that's how we talked, in terms of which of us would be the one to lead the Conservative party when the time came.'[10] In any case, those arrested were released the next day without charges.[11] Bullingdon members didn't have their careers inconvenienced by youthful criminal records.

Still, the Bullingdon 'haunted me for most of my political life', wrote Cameron in his post-prime-ministerial memoir: 'When I look now at the much-reproduced photograph taken of our group of appallingly over-self-confident "sons of privilege", I cringe.' He added, in mitigation: 'These were also the years after the ITV adaptation of *Brideshead Revisited*, when quite a few of us were carried away by the fantasy of an Evelyn Waugh-like Oxford existence.'[12]

Johnson once said he was 'embarrassed' to have been a member, and called the Bullingdon 'a truly shameful vignette of almost superhuman undergraduate arrogance, toffishness and twittishness'.[13] On the other hand, he added: 'But at the time you felt it was wonderful to be going round swanking it up.'[14]

He did the Bullingdon like he did everything else: ironically. When he visited China as mayor of London in 2013, the mayor of Beijing, Wang Anshun, reminisced to him about his own time studying at Oxford: 'Every night we would have a banquet session and at the end we would all sing songs. It was a very happy time.' Johnson, no doubt thinking of 'Buller' days, replied, 'The Chancellor and I used to do that, too.' Osborne was visiting China that same week, the two Bullingdon members representing Britain simultaneously, though very much not together.[15]

It is understandable that the all-male, toff, de facto networking society has come to be seen as the nursery bed of future power. The Bullingdon certainly did help reinforce ties from schooldays. However, it was fairly marginal to the Oxford Tories' university lives. Johnson didn't like losing control through drink,[16] while Cameron was a cautious type, who appears to have joined chiefly because he is by nature a joiner who tries not to give offence.

Cameron was unusual among Oxford Tories in that he barely spent any time at university building career networks. 'I feel awful saying that, but I literally don't remember meeting him once,' says Rachel Johnson, his contemporary. He got his First, followed the TV shows *Neighbours* and *Going for Gold*,[17] had girlfriends, met middle-class people for the first time, amused himself in dining clubs, and held a celebratory party in his rooms after Thatcher's election victory in 1987,[18] but didn't do anything so vulgar as burnish his CV with student politics. He recalled,

I hardly took part. My fascination with politics was developing, but for some reason I didn't want to play at it. I visited the Oxford Union a few times, and saw stars like Boris Johnson, already a very funny speaker, and masters of debate like Nick Robinson, who would later become political editor of the BBC.[19]

Cameron must have sensed that it would be easy enough to catch up later. After all, he was distantly related to the Queen, his father chaired the establishment club White's (a Bullingdon for grown-ups), and his cousin Ferdinand Mount headed Thatcher's Number Ten Policy Unit. Cameron's future passage into the Tory party was assured.

Networking at Oxford was for a parvenu like Johnson, whose father had only been to the lesser boarding school of Sherborne. Johnson was an example of the coalition that makes up the British elite: the core of hereditaries is supplemented by upper-middle-class strivers and a few invitees from the lower orders.

Johnson understood that he had to build his political career on a more consequential stage than the Bullingdon: the Oxford Union. As Jan Morris gloated, accurately: 'There is probably nowhere on earth where so many men have learnt how to be politicians.'[20]

5

THE CHILDREN'S PARLIAMENT

The Union occupies a special place in the history of our nation.
Harold Macmillan[1]

At *Cherwell*, we were always writing about the Union. The debating society, founded in 1823, based in a court- yard behind the Cornmarket shopping street, was a kind of children's House of Commons. Like its London model, it resembled a gentlemen's club complete with reading rooms, writing room and bar, and, across the garden, Europe's largest purpose-built debating chamber.[2] The Union was one of those Oxford institutions that can flat- ter middle-class teenagers like William Hague and Theresa May into feeling posh. Union officers wore white tie, speak- ers black tie, and everyone called each other 'honourable member'. The walls were lined with busts of former prime ministers who had been Union men. Nineteen-year-olds debated visiting sixty-year-old cabinet ministers, and tried to loll on the front benches just like them. Christopher Hollis, in his 1965 book on the Union, called the place 'a parody of the Parliament of 1864 rather than that of 1964'.[3]

It hadn't changed much by the 1980s. I never became

a member but I sometimes got press tickets to debates, and I remember a young Binyamin Netanyahu despatching hecklers, and, on the fiftieth anniversary of Dunkirk, Ted Heath evoking Oxford in 1940 when German invasion loomed. Heath had been elected Union president in November 1938 after accusing Neville Chamberlain of 'turning all four cheeks to Hitler at once'.[4]

Another attraction of the Union was the bar, which – almost miraculously in 1980s Britain – stayed open into the early morning after debates, until the deferential local police finally intervened. By the mid 1980s the Union also had a comedy club in its Jazz Cellar, where an undergraduate comedian named Armando Iannucci – who would go on to create the satirical TV series *The Thick of It* and *Veep* – was learning the art of mocking politicians.[5]

The Union (as well as the PPE degree) is a large part of the explanation for why Oxford produces so many prime ministers. From the beginning, the chamber had functioned as a self-conscious nursery of the Commons, dominated by Etonians.[6] In 1831, Gladstone had made such a powerful anti-reform speech at the Union that a friend from Eton alerted his father, the Duke of Newcastle, who offered the twenty-two-year-old prodigy one of the parliamentary pocket boroughs in his gift.[7] In 1853 Edward Bradley watched 'beardless gentlemen … juggle the same tricks of rhetoric as their fathers were doing in certain other debates in a certain other House'.[8]

The Etonian Macmillan, who was elected Librarian of the Union just before the First World War broke out, recollected in old age:

The Union was fun because it was an opportunity to learn something of the parliamentary system, to which I always had ambitions. It was organised like the House of Commons. The President, like the Speaker, was in the chair. You addressed the chair. There were front benches and back benches and so forth.[9]

The Union's debating rules were modelled on those of the Commons. Opposing speakers sat facing each other in adversarial formation, and there was the same 'telling' of Ayes and Noes. 'In 1941,' writes David Walter in his history of the place, 'the Union offered its despatch boxes to the House of Commons to replace those which had been lost in the bombing, and of which they were copies'.[10]

But unlike the Commons, the Union had no actual power. Almost the only thing the Union president could actually do was stage debates. Naturally, then, the Union encouraged a focus on rhetoric over policy. The institution was of a piece with Oxford's tutorials and the university's social language of ironic banter: it perfected the articulacy that enabled aspiring politicians, barristers and columnists to argue any case, whether they believed it or not. In the Union, a speaker might prepare one side of a debate, and then on the day suddenly have to switch to the other side to replace an opponent who had dropped out.[11] I suspect it was this rhetorical tradition that prompted Louis Mac-Neice to write, in 1939:

> ... I hasten to explain
> That having once been to the University of Oxford
> You can never really again

Believe anything that anyone says and that of course
  is an asset
In a world like ours[12]

At speakers' dinners, twenty-year-old Union hacks min-
gled with political powerbrokers up from London. Heath
first met Churchill as a student in 1936, chatting until 2 a.m.
over a nightcap in the Oxford rooms of Churchill's pal,
Frederick Lindemann.[13] On another of Churchill's visits to
the Union, he remarked to a student (who happened to be
the future Tory minister Quintin Hogg): 'If you can speak
in this country, you can do anything.'[14]

In the late 1960s, the young debater Christopher Hitchens recalled having the chance

> ... to meet senior ministers and parliamentarians 'up
> close' and dine with them before as well as drink with
> them afterward, and be amazed once again at how
> ignorant and sometimes plain stupid were the people
> who claimed to run the country. This was an essential
> stage of my formation and one for which I am hugely
> grateful ...[15]

Some of the London powerbrokers acted as talent scouts,
and ambitious undergraduates took advantage.

The Union was a reason for politically inclined students,
especially Tory public schoolboys, to choose Oxford over
Cambridge. When I asked Dan Hannan why so many of
today's politicians were at Oxford, he replied, 'It's been true
forever, right? ... I guess people who were very interested
in politics were more likely to apply to Oxford, because

they think there's more going on there.' By contrast, the Cambridge Union has never produced a British prime minister. An attendee at one of its recent reunions reports 'a room full of failed ambition and putting a hearty face on'.

At Oxford, the Union's ceaseless debates and election campaigns kept the university buzzing with politics. British governments face elections every five years, but the Union elected a president, secretary, treasurer and librarian every eight-week term. The anthropologist Fiona Graham, in her 2005 ethnography of the Union, described some students as 'virtually professional politicians, complete with support staff and intricate election strategies and meetings'.[16]

Nearly all campaigning for votes was supposedly banned under the Union's own Rule 33. There were occasional attempts to enforce the rule, through tribunals featuring London lawyers, but candidates almost always flouted it. Union politicians, known as 'hacks' – instantly recognisable because they were the only students who wore suits – were forever traipsing around the colleges tapping up ordinary students with the phrase, 'May I count on your vote?' Typically, though, only a few hundred people, many of them Union insiders, bothered to cast theirs.[17]

Allied candidates organised themselves into 'slates', the Union version of parties but with the ideology usually left out.[18] The slates were illegal, semi-secret, mostly hidden from the electorate, and essential to the whole enterprise. Entirely against the rules, candidates would campaign for their slates: 'Vote for me as treasurer, for him as secretary and for her as president.' In other words, cheating was built into the system.

The slates made a Union election look like a team game, but really it was an individual sport. Almost every 'hack' was in it chiefly for themselves. Slates offered endless opportunities for betrayal: a candidate might defect from one slate days before the election to join the rival faction, letting down people who might be close friends or lovers. There were rarely any lasting hard feelings: one term later, traitor and betrayed might team up on a new slate. The atmosphere was suffused with an amateurish ruthlessness.

A 'Union career' was good practice for Westminster. You learned when an ostensible ally was lying to your face, or when you should be lying to his; when it was safe to break a rule, and when it wasn't.[19] Radek Sikorski says it was at the Union 'where I first learned expressions such as "knifing" and "hacking"'.[20] Outcomes were brutal and public: when Evelyn Waugh stood for secretary, he finished sixth and last.[21] The traditional climax of a Union election was one Etonian backstabbing another for the presidency. Michael Heseltine, who had occupied the president's chair – which sat on a raised dais like a throne – called it 'the first step to being prime minister'. Once you had ascended the Union, Downing Street felt within your grasp.

Politicos at Oxford formed a tight-knit little universe. In 1976, Theresa Brasier and her future husband Philip May, both of them Union 'hacks', were introduced at a disco of the Oxford University Conservative Association (OUCA) by another Union president, Benazir Bhutto, then already preparing to be prime minister of Pakistan. Brasier held similar ambitions, even if none of her contemporaries seems to have realised. The broadcaster Michael Crick, who was Union president in 1979, says:

Theresa May was a pretty good speaker, and when she was relaxed she could be very funny. But she is very buttoned-up and hidden. You never really got to know Theresa. Everyone in Oxford politics who is described as knowing Theresa – even Damian Green – will say, 'I've never really known her.' The whole of my generation are agreed that Theresa May is the last person we would have expected to become prime minister. She was the least able at outward political skills.

Instead, adds Crick, contemporaries would have tipped Green, Alan Duncan, Colin Moynihan or Daniel (now Baron) Moylan. Their machinations for power were mocked in the Oxford satirical magazine *Passing Wind*, edited by the undergraduate Ian Hislop, future editor of *Private Eye*.

The future Australian prime minister Malcolm Turnbull met both his future counterparts Brasier and Bhutto at the Union, the first time in 1977 when he came to town as a visiting debater, and ended up giving Bhutto a lift back to London. 'I have to say I've never known anyone drape themselves across the back seat of a Mini Minor as elegantly as she did.'

A year later Turnbull returned to Oxford as a Rhodes Scholar. Crick found him 'the most dynamic person I ever met at Oxford, or since really'.

What was Turnbull's impression of Oxford?

It was the first place that anyone asked me essentially, 'What does your father do?' People actually were hung up on how they spoke, their social background, where they went to school and so forth. I'm not saying these distinctions don't exist in Australia, but they're on the margins of the margins in Australia compared to the United Kingdom when I was there.

Turnbull spoke occasionally at Union debates, and intervened in the life of Theresa Brasier, as he would discover half a lifetime later at the G20 meetings in Hangzhou, China in 2016. 'She said, in a bilateral with about thirty people around the table, "Oh, Philip [May]'s never forgotten that advice you gave him at Oxford." And of course I had no recollection whatsoever what it had been. It turned out that apparently I had told him to stop hesitating and get on and propose to her.'

What had Turnbull made of the Oxford Union?

It's standard student politics, which is all about getting to the top of the greasy pile ... student politics is all about the game. And I think it's fair to say that some people who go from being involved in student politics into real politics are more enamored of the game than they are of what should be the objective of politics, which is good public policy. The Union is less a forum for debating the big issues of the day than it is of being an entertaining speaker.

6

THE BOUNDER SPEAKS

*Charm is the great English blight. It does not
exist outside these damp islands. It spots and kills
anything it touches. It kills love; it kills art ...'*
Anthony Blanche in *Brideshead Revisited*[1]

Like his role model Churchill, Boris Johnson spent years
mastering the ancient craft of public speaking.[2] Eton had
offered unmatched opportunities to practise. Johnson ran
the school's Debating Society, and by the time he left was
so well-versed in traditional speech-making that he could
perform it as parody. His sister Rachel says:

Eton Debating Society, PolSoc [Eton's Political
Society] all those places honed your oratorical abilities
at a young age. They were given a huge head start,
these guys. You'd get incredible heavy-hitters going to
address PolSoc and talking to the boys.
It's like playing tennis – you can't pick up a tennis
racket and go and walk on Centre Court and expect to
beat Roger Federer. So much of all these things are practice. You learn what lands, and you learn what doesn't.

And I think the problem is that women are frightened
of trying and failing and being seen to try and fail.

Johnson learned at school to defeat opponents whose arguments were better simply by ignoring their arguments. He
discovered how to win elections and debates not by boring
the audience with detail, but with carefully timed jokes,
calculated lowerings of voice, and ad hominem jibes.

He went up to Oxford in 1983 as a vessel of focused
ambition. Ironic about everything else, he was serious
about himself. Within his peer group of public schoolboys,
he felt like a poor man in a hurry. He started university
with three aims, writes Sonia Purnell in *Just Boris*: to get a
first-class degree, to find a wife (his own parents had met at
Oxford), and to become Union president. At university he
was always 'thinking two decades ahead', says his Oxford
friend Lloyd Evans.[3]

Whereas most students arrived in Oxford barely
knowing the Union existed, Johnson possessed the savvy
of his class: his father had come to Oxford in 1959 intend-
ing to become Union president. Stanley Johnson had failed,
but his son was a star. Eton encourages boys to develop
their individuality, or at least craft an individual brand,
and nobody had done this more fully than Johnson. Simon
Veksner, who followed him from their house at Eton to
the Union, recalls: 'Boris's charisma even then was off the
charts, you couldn't measure it: so funny, warm, charming, self-deprecating. You put on a funny act, based on the
Beano and P. G. Wodehouse. It works, and then that is
who you are.'

Johnson became the character he played. He turned

self-parody into a form of self-promotion. Like many British displays of eccentricity, his shambolic hair and dress were class statements. Much like Sebastian Flyte's teddy bear in *Brideshead Revisited*, they said: my privileged status is so secure that I am free to defy norms.

At Oxford, Johnson merged three archetypes from British popular culture: Brideshead, Wooster and the boarding-school bounder. The bounder is the rogue of his school, who doesn't do his 'prep', smokes behind the rugger field, breaks bounds, romances girls and is always getting into 'scrapes'. In adulthood, bounders traditionally end up hiding from their creditors in Australia.

Johnson got off to the perfect start with his marriage ambitions: he acquired as his university girlfriend the posh and beautiful Allegra Mostyn-Owen, the Alpha female of their cohort. *Cherwell*, in an impressive scoop, managed to announce their engagement two and a half years before they actually married.[4] Good-looking himself and regularly covered in student newspapers, Johnson became an 'Oxford character', one of the few undergraduates known beyond his immediate circle. Already, then, he possessed the political asset of being all too easy to write about.

Mostyn-Owen's elite entrées supplemented Johnson's own. She introduced him to the journalist Tina Brown, who was visiting Oxford to write about the death from a heroin overdose of the upper-class socialite Olivia Channon. Brown reports being traduced by Johnson, who supposedly ghosted an inaccurate attack on her in the *Telegraph*, under Mostyn-Owen's byline. Brown claims to have recorded in her contemporaneous diary: 'Boris Johnson is an epic shit. I hope he ends badly.'[5]

Toby Young remembers the first time he saw Johnson speak at the Union, in October 1983:

> The motion was deadly serious – 'This House Would Reintroduce Capital Punishment' – yet almost everything that came out of his mouth provoked gales of laughter. This was no ordinary undergraduate proposing a motion, but a Music Hall veteran performing a well-rehearsed comic routine. His lack of preparedness seemed less like evidence of his own shortcomings as a debater and more a way of sending up all the other speakers, as well as the pomposity of the proceedings.

To Young, another who had come up to Oxford with his head full of *Brideshead Revisited* (the TV version), Johnson represented 'the "real" Oxford, the Platonic ideal.'[6] He admits, 'I was completely swept up by the Boris cult.'[7] Johnson, he said, 'was the Biggest Man on Campus. He was the silverback gorilla, the alpha male.'[8]

One young debating hopeful of the day was Frank Luntz, the future American pollster who has become known as a master of political language. A self-proclaimed 'word guy', Luntz invented the phrase 'climate change' for the George W. Bush administration so as to make 'global warming' seem innocuous (something he now says he regrets).[9] He recalls:

> Boris was brilliant. He bumbles through the details but God does he know the substance. I had never met anyone like him, and I still haven't. Boris gave a speech on the Middle East – it's the best Middle East speech to

this day I've ever heard, because he talked about it in terms of a playground, and kids attacking the little kid on the playground. Boris created a brilliant metaphor and then made the argument around that.

Johnson also benefited from the quality of debating competition, says Luntz: 'I've never seen a class of more talented people than that class of 1984–86 at the Oxford Union. I was twenty-two when I got there and I looked up to people who were eighteen or nineteen years old, because of their talent.' Luntz singles out Nick Robinson, Simon Stevens and Michael Gove. He told me:

Any one of those three, when they rose [in a debate] to intervene, the entire chamber shut up, there wasn't a sound, because everyone knew that when they were recognised, the [previous speaker] was dead, because they were so incisive. Just bring in the ambulance and take out the body, because the three of them could cut you up and show you your heart before you collapsed. We can't do that in America, nobody can.

If you made a good argument but you didn't have the backing for it, you were so embarrassed that you couldn't show yourself at the bar after the debate. If you didn't have the facts, if you didn't know the counterarguments, they would figure it out and destroy you. You had to know everything because you had no idea what was going to come at you – and it came at you during your speech.

It's the most wonderful [speaking] style ever. It's like a mental massage. Oxford was the perfect training ground. It trained them because they were surrounded by people who were just as talented as they were, just as career-driven as they were, they were surrounded by thousands of *them*.

Anthony Gardner, another American contemporary of Johnson's, later US ambassador to the EU, was less impressed:

> Boris was an accomplished performer in the Oxford Union where a premium was placed on rapier wit rather than any fidelity to the facts. It was a perfect training ground for those planning to be professional amateurs. I recall how many poor American students were skewered during debates when they rather plod.dingly read out statistics; albeit accurate and often relevant in their argumentation, they would be jeered by the crowds with cries of 'boring' or 'facts'![10]

Politically, Johnson shared with most Oxford Tories of his generation a generalised faith in Thatcherism. The prime minister in her 1982–87 heyday, their formative political years, was a role model. She instinctively chose the uncompromising solution. She steamrollered all opponents, from Tory 'Wets' to Argentinian conscripts. She stood for unabashed material advancement for the winners, and a world in which Britain could still make the rules through willpower alone.[11] After her death in 2013, Johnson would call on Oxford to endow a new Thatcher College. 'Why not have a college in honour of their greatest post-war benefactress as they rake in the doubloons from international student fees?' he asked.[12]

The undergraduate Johnson quickly became king of all he surveyed. In 1984, a sixth-former named Damian Furniss came to Johnson's college Balliol for his entrance interview. 'I was a rural working-class kid with a stammer from a state school which hadn't prepared me for the experience,' Furniss would recall in 2019.

> My session with the dons was scheduled for first thing after breakfast, meaning I was staying the night and had an evening to kill in the college bar. Johnson was propping up with his coterie of acolytes whose only apparent role in life was to laugh at his jokes. Three years older than me ... you'd have expected him to play the ambassador role, welcoming an aspiring member of his college ... Instead, his piss-taking was brutal. In the course of the pint I felt obliged to finish he mocked my speech impediment, my accent, my school, my dress sense, my haircut, my background, my father's work as farm worker and garage proprietor, and my prospects in the scholarship interview I was there for. His only motivation was to amuse his posh boy mates.

At around the time of this encounter, Johnson was running for Union president against the grammar-school boy Neil Sherlock. The election dramatised Oxford's class struggle: toff versus 'stain'. Sherlock, later a partner at KPMG and PwC, and briefly a special adviser to the Liberal deputy prime minister Nick Clegg, was the first in his family to attend university.[13] He says that when he arrived at Oxford, 'I'd never seen a debate in my life. I'd never seen anyone in black tie, let alone in white tie.'

He recalls: 'Boris Mark I was a very conventional Tory, clearly on the right, and had what I would term an Old Etonian entitlement view: "I should get the top job because I'm standing for the top job." He didn't have a good sense of what he was going to do with it.'

Allegra invited Sherlock to tea and asked him not to stand against 'my Boris'. Undeterred, Sherlock campaigned on a platform of 'meritocrat versus toff, competence versus incompetence'. Johnson mobilised his public-school networks (he seemed short of close friends) but even the 150 or so Etonians up at Oxford at the time[14] proved too small a political base in the new mass Union.

Johnson's candidacy also suffered from his Toryism. Conservatives may have been the largest faction within the Union, but they were a minority in the university as a whole. Most Oxford dons of the time were anti-Thatcher, too. Denying her an honorary degree in 1985 to protest her cuts to education and research was the university's seminal political statement of the decade. 'Why should we feed the hand that bites us?' asked one don.[15] Luntz recalls that Oxford considered Thatcher 'the most evil living person on the face of the earth'. He himself felt he was socially excluded for speaking for her.

(Largely for that reason, Luntz told me, with the 'radical candour' he has adopted since having a stroke in 2020: 'I actually hated my three years there. I don't have a warm place in my heart for it at all. If you said to me, what in your life would you do over?, that's number one.' However, he blames himself. 'I blew it', he says, for having been 'tone-deaf' to the prevailing mood. He dictated a sentence that he wanted me to include in the book: 'Luntz was emphatic that he took responsibility for his experiences.' Still, after returning to the US, he launched his polling career off the Oxford brand. When we talked on Zoom, he moved his camera around to show me his vast, messy bedroom: 'I have really cool shit here. I've had a really interesting life. I hated Oxford, but Oxford made my life possible.' Didn't he think he would have become a leading pollster even without Oxford? 'No, I don't.')

In the Union election, Sherlock beat Johnson, and came away underwhelmed by his opponent: 'The rhetoric, the personality, the wit were rather randomly deployed, beyond getting a laugh.' Sherlock expected OUCA's president Nick Robinson to become the political star, and Johnson to become a 'rather good journalist'. Instead, Robinson went on to present the *Today* programme (where in October 2021 he told a verbose Johnson, 'Prime minister, stop talking)'.[16]

The emotional intensity of a Union election is extraordinary: betrayals abound, participants are at their most sensitive phase of adult life, and nobody is getting much sleep. The candidates are running for the most prestigious post any of them will have ever held at that point in their lives – and quite likely the most prestigious the winner will ever hold. Losers often burst into tears. They feel that their very essence has been rejected, not just whatever political views they might (or might not) hold. Johnson's defeat to Sherlock wounded him, and he learned from it. 'It was, quite likely, the making of him as a politician,' writes Purnell. 'It taught him the unassailable truth that no one can truly succeed in politics if he relies entirely on his own cadre.'[17]

But Etonians tend to get second chances, and a year after his humiliation, he ran for president again. He had absorbed another truth: that personality could trump politics. The second time around, he disguised his Toryism by presenting himself as an unthreatening funny man – 'centrist, social democrat, warm and cuddly', sums up Sherlock. He even managed to forge an alliance with a Union hack from Ruskin College, and rallied its student body of mostly adult working-class trade unionists behind his slate. *Cherwell*'s diarist John Evelyn mock-praised 'Balliol's blond bombshell' as 'the unstoppable force for Socialist in the Palace of the People debating society (the Union to you) ... Who can stop our Old Etonian Leninist from stamping his personal hammer and sickle all over the Union?'[18] Thrown in among leftists and liberals, Johnson learned to flourish by spoofing himself. 'He got away with being a Tory by being funny,' says his sister Rachel.

And why not? Since the Union president couldn't make policy even about students' lives, and Johnson wasn't very interested in policy anyway, it was all just a power game. Johnson's second presidential campaign was more competent. Luntz – earning his first-ever consulting fee, of £180[19] – conducted a poll for Johnson in which, as Luntz recalls, almost all the questions were about students' sexual habits. He says now: 'My mother was so embarrassed because it made *The New York Times*. She said, "How dare you ask people those questions?"'

But in fact, the sex was just a cover, says Luntz: 'I knew it would be so controversial that no one would think, "Actually this was a poll done for a political campaign".' He slipped in two questions about the Union that were intended to identify which candidate Johnson should strike a deal with about trading second-preference votes.

In this second campaign, Johnson also worked his charm beyond his base. Gove, a fresher in 1985, told Johnson's biographer, Andrew Gimson: 'The first time I saw him was in the Union bar ... He seemed like a kindly, Oxford character, but he was really there like a great basking shark waiting for freshers to swim towards him.' Gove, who campaigned for him, admits: 'I was Boris's stooge.' And then, using the same phrase as Toby Young: 'I became a votary of the Boris cult.'[20]

Johnson's persona was the perfect vehicle for a slate. In the English context, it seemed right and just that the highest political office should go to the most charismatic Etonian of his day. With the votaries assuming their natural places around him, he won the presidency. Johnson's defeated opponent Mark Carnegie later reflected: 'Sure he's engaging, but this guy is an absolute fucking killer.'[21]

That was what it took. As Toby Young wrote in the Union's house magazine in 1985: 'It doesn't matter how unpopular you are with the establishment, how stupid you are, how small your College is or how pretentious your old school: if only you've got the sheer will you can succeed.' The types who succeeded in the Union, Young explained, were people who 'when confronted with any social environment ... perceive only the hierarchical conditions which determine people's status within it; and they have no means of relating to other individuals other than as tools and enemies.'

Young wrote that it was lucky that that Union existed – 'that in an environment as full of ruthless, sociopathic people as Oxford, there should be an institution that sucks them all in, contains all their wilful energy and grants them power only over each other.' He concluded his article: 'Let us hope with all our hearts that today's Union Presidents will become tomorrow's MPs, Cabinet members and Prime Ministers for then, like today, we will at least know where they are.'[22]

Johnson's gift turned out to be for winning office, not doing anything with it. He didn't make much of his presidency, recalls Tim Hames, a Union politician of the time: 'The thing was a shambles. He couldn't organise a term card to save his life. He didn't have the sort of support mechanism that he realised in later life that he required.'

Once elected, Johnson also dropped his centrist disguise. When Balliol's Master Anthony Kenny was contacted by a Social Democratic Party MP who needed an intern, Kenny replied: 'I've just the man for you. Bright and witty and with suitable political views. He's just finished being president of the Union, and his name is Boris Johnson.' But when Kenny told Johnson about the job, he laughed: 'Master, don't you know I am a dyed-in-the-wool Tory?'[23]

★

After graduation, Johnson wrote a telling essay on Oxford politics for his sister's *The Oxford Myth*.[24] He starts, characteristically, by stating the case against the Union:

> Nothing but a massage-parlour for the egos of the assorted twits, twerps, toffs and misfits that inhabit it

... To many undergraduates, the Union niffs of the purest, most naked politics, stripped of all issues except personality and ambition ... Ordinary punters are frequently discouraged from voting by this thought: are they doing anything else but fattening the CVs of those who get elected?

Still, he noted, the glittering prizes of London were within easy reach: 'The best way to get an idea of the importance of the Oxford Union in British political life is to spend a quarter of an hour looking at the standing committee photographs as they wend back up the stairs and the landing to the beginning of the century.' He critiques the undergraduate appearances of various future stars ('Benazir Bhutto wears very odd dresses ... Heath looks fat') before ending with the chosen role model: 'As we near the top of the stairs, we see a very youthful figure sitting cross-legged at the front of the group, like the scorer in the school cricket team. He looks about thirteen. He is Harold Macmillan.'

His essay then tackles the great question: how to set about becoming the next Macmillan? Well, even if you speak like Cicero, you will never get electoral success 'without first grasping and mastering the principles of hacking'. Johnson advises student politicians to assemble 'a disciplined and deluded collection of stooges' to get out the vote. 'Lonely girls from the women's colleges, very often scientists' were particularly useful:

With their fresh complexions and flowery flocks, they are the prototypes of local Conservative Party workers. Brisk, stern, running to fat, but backing their

largely male candidates with a porky decisiveness ...
For these young women in their structured world of
molecules and quarks, machine politics offers human
friction and warmth.

Johnson in this passage is reflecting on the first society he
had encountered in which women played some role in
power structures. Reading it, you realise why almost all
Union presidents who become Tory politicians are men
(and arts graduates).

Johnson added: 'The tragedy of the stooge is that ...
he wants so much to believe that his relationship with the
candidate is special that he shuts out the truth. The terrible
art of the candidate is to coddle the self-deception of the
stooge.'

7

STOOGES, VOTARIES AND VICTIMS

We on this side know each other.

Jacob Rees-Mogg explaining why Conservative MPs did not need
to wear face masks in the House of Commons, October 2021[1]

Scanning *Cherwell*'s John Evelyn column of 15 November
1985, you find much of Britain's right wing of the 2020s
already in place. Beside the story about the 'Old Etonian
Leninist' Johnson, another item, headed 'Who Thinks
They're Who', mocks Johnson's girlfriend Allegra and
Toby Young, 'Oxford's answer to the gutter press'.[2] And
on the other side of the Johnson item, Evelyn introduces
his readers to an eighteen-year-old Aberdonian politico
named Michael Gove, already gaining fame at Oxford
barely a month after his arrival. 'Michael conceals his
rabidly reactionary political views under a Jane Austen
cleric-like exterior,' writes Evelyn, who then swerves into
uncharacteristic generosity: 'The worst thing about this
precocious pin-up is that he is, in fact, disgustingly unambi-
tious and talented: Watch this space for stories of eventual
corruption ...'[3]

Gove's Scottish parents had both left school at fifteen,

but they sent him to an Aberdonian private day school. He arrived at Oxford wearing a young-fogey uniform of green tweed suit (bought at the Salvation Army for £1.50) and a red tie.[4] Because he still had to build his confidence and network, he needed the Union more than the Etonians did. It was new terrain for him, but one to which he was perfectly adapted. *Cherwell* called him 'the best debater in the Union'.[5] He could even make a compelling case to a student audience against free choice in sexual behaviour.[6]

One contemporary recalls a standard opening joke of his: 'As I was telling my Fillipino manservant this morning … '[7] Gove wore a kilt in debates[8] and enjoyed the ritual joke about whether he was wearing anything underneath. He plunged into Oxford's public life: in 1987, *Cherwell* reported him paying £6 for the Union president, Jessica Pulay, at the Union's 'slave auction', 'an opportunity to buy your favourite Union person for the evening'. Gove himself attracted 'enthusiastic bidding' at £35, while Boris Johnson was sold in absentia.[9] (Inevitably, Pulay became an establishment figure herself, with leading roles at various investment banks, the UK Debt Management Office and as a trustee of the English National Opera.)

Gove grew into a recognisable Oxford character in outsized glasses, speaking with an exaggerated oratorical air even in daily life. When the future *Guardian* journalist Luke Harding arrived at Oxford in 1987, Gove led his freshers' tour of the Union. 'He was basically the same [as in 2021],' recalls Harding. 'He had this preternatural self-confidence, this faux-courtly manner. He seemed somewhat parodic, someone who wasn't going to flourish in the real world.'

One friend who has known Gove since Oxford says: 'He'd find it quite understandable that you found him ridiculous and bizarre, and he'd continued to be very polite to you.' This is a consistent theme in testimonies about Gove, Rees-Mogg and Hannan: even their political enemies agree on their friendliness. (Johnson is something of an exception: perhaps he has always been so high-status that he has had to pretend to camaraderie only at moments of crisis.) Gove et al. seemed to show genuine interest in the person talking to them, and not just be looking over their shoulder for someone more important. No wonder, because for all the popular prejudice against politicians, it's a job in which likeability is an almost essential quality. Perhaps the Oxford Tories became politicians because they were naturally friendly types, or perhaps they learned to treat people nicely because they were always on the hunt for votes.

Gove was unusually ideological by Union standards, a Thatcherite meritocrat who already knew what he thought. A Union contemporary recalls that though Gove wasn't 'on the loony "Abolish the NHS" fringe', 'he was the kind of guy who would come up with an amazing argument for using nuclear weapons.'

In 1987, Gove wrote a short essay on schooling for the Union's house magazine. It opens with a puerile yet complicated joke about Oscar Wilde, but then he gets stuck in. He takes a swipe at the then education secretary, 'spiv-like' Kenneth Baker, but has clearly been influenced by the Thatcherite ideal of a return to Victorian excellence. The twenty-year-old's arguments offer a detailed preview of his tenure as education secretary from 2010 to 2014:

- British schools should set clear, demanding standards that pupils must meet. 'If we can teach lower primates to read and write, why can we not ensure a somewhat higher standard of achievement for our own children?'
- 'Core curricula? Yes, we need to pass on certain basic skills and knowledge and avoid time-wasting exercises in irrelevancies'
- 'Testing at regular stages? Yes'
- Teachers' pay should be tied to performance
- 'Opting out, privatisation, parental choice' could all help change schools 'from producer- to consumer-oriented organisations.'[10]

Elsewhere, in a paean to an elitism of excellence in the Union's house magazine, he warned: 'I cannot over-emphasise what elitism is *not*. It is not about back-slapping cliques, reactionary chic or Old Etonian egos. It is a spirit of unashamed glamour, excitement and competition … We are all here, part of an elite. It is our duty to bear that in mind.'[11]

There was already in the young Gove a tension that would persist: the clever Thatcherite outsider's contempt for ancestral upper-class English privilege, combined with an eagerness to acquire its trappings. As Union president in 1988, he defended the wearing of white and black ties in debates. 'Some people might be scared and intimidated by it,' he admitted, 'but what you lose there you gain in a sense of occasion.'[12]

*

For ambitious Tories who weren't brilliant speakers, or whose energies couldn't entirely be contained within the Union, there was another route to Westminster: the Oxford University Conservative Association. Its past presidents included Heath, Thatcher, William Rees-Mogg (father of Jacob), William Hague and his Oxford crony Guy Hands, the future investor, while Theresa Brasier had been a committee member. Unlike Union hacks, some OUCA and Labour Club officers actually gained a little political experience of ordinary Britain: during general elections, they would go canvassing in working-class Oxford.

Margaret Roberts (the future Thatcher) had to channel her political ambitions into OUCA because the Union of her day banned women. After she became president in 1946, *Isis* magazine remarked that the 'Conservative Association under the queenly sway of Margaret Roberts is at the height of its post-war boom'. During her reign, OUCA's membership rose well above 1,000 for the first time since the 1920s.

Roberts seems to have enjoyed being surrounded by posh male Tories, but one OUCA contemporary recalls that they 'merely tolerated' her as a 'slogger', 'someone who could be relied on to do the donkey work'.[13] David Blair (a former OUCA president himself, now Boris Johnson's speechwriter) writes in his history of OUCA: 'Under her influence, OUCA embraced the new realistic Toryism, personified by Rab Butler, which accepted much of what Attlee's Labour government had done ... It is ironic that a political career which would reach a climax with battles against the post-war consensus began with an accommodation to them.' Edward Boyle succeeded Thatcher as

OUCA president; in 1967, when he resigned from Heath's shadow cabinet, she replaced him as shadow education secretary.[14]

By the late 1980s, OUCA had acquired (at least by Johnson's calculation) 1,800 members.[15] *Cherwell* called it 'the largest students' political society in Western Europe'.[16] Its recruitment slogan was 'Be a socialite, not a socialist'.[17]

The association's president in 1987 was Jeremy Hunt. Tim Hames sums up: 'The Boris appeal was Boris. Michael was interested in ideology and ideas. Jeremy was more a small-c managerial conservative.' Hunt was neither charismatic nor eloquent, and had no obvious political passions, but he was the archetypal head boy (a role he'd held at Charterhouse). His father, noted *Cherwell*, 'wields some pretty persuasive firepower; he is Admiral Hunt, the man with his finger on the Polaris button'.[18]

Tall and courteous, another distant relative of the Queen, Hunt at Oxford tried to rise above Tory factionalism. OUCA at the time was divided between Thatcherites (mostly state-school boys) and Heathite 'Wets' (tweedy public schoolboys), who liked to exchange arcane factional insults. Hunt saw it as his mission to unite everybody. After *Cherwell* reported that a 'libertarian faction' was trying to 'take over' OUCA, and that one committee member was a 'Moonie' (a member of the Unification Church cult), Hunt wrote a letter to the editor, in a formal register rarely seen in *Cherwell*: 'OUCA remains a moderate association controlled by neither libertarians nor any other faction within the Conservative Party, and exists to represent the views of all Conservative students at Oxford.' The Moonie, he added, had been expelled.[19]

Standards seem to have slipped after Hunt's day. In 1989, the University proctors briefly removed OUCA's official recognition when the association ('with true entrepreneurial spirit', wrote Hannan) organised a fundraising cabaret at which a male and female stripper used marshmallows to simulate sex acts, in front of a disappointingly small audience of thirty people.[20]

*

Like most boys of his social class, Jacob Rees-Mogg had been trained since early childhood above all to speak and write well. Owen Matthews, his contemporary at Westminster Under School, remembers him, aged about eleven or twelve – 'exactly the same as Jacob aged fifty-one' – addressing the assembled pupils on the topic of cruelty to animals. So ridiculously plummy did his voice seem even in that setting, and so parodically adult was his delivery, that the entire school burst out laughing. Rees-Mogg plugged on unfazed and finished his speech, earning an ovation for his pluck. It was precious training. At Eton he joined the debating society, and set up the Stockton Society, which once persuaded the Earl of Stockton himself, Harold Macmillan, to come and speak.

Rees-Mogg wasn't ancestrally posh. Instead he 'adopted the persona of the institutions he attended,' diagnoses Matthews, who believes that this began as a defence mechanism for a thin bookish child. Arriving at Oxford in 1988, he instantly became an unmissable sight, a rail-thin teenager promenading along Broad Street dressed like a Victorian vicar, in a double-breasted suit with an umbrella.

In that time and place, it was about the most unconventional outfit imaginable, stranger than, say, punk gear. I asked him in 2021 whether he hadn't felt self-conscious in it. 'I didn't think through an image,' he replied. 'Indeed, no one with any sense would ever have thought of the image that I had at Oxford.' But when I asked another Etonian to decode the message of Rees-Mogg's university get-up, he explained: 'It's saying, "I belong to another club to the one you're in, and it's a better club".'

Nearly forty years earlier, Rees-Mogg's father William had himself been a throwback in 1950s Oxford, known as 'the oldest young man in captivity'.[21] His clothes 'would not have disgraced a Victorian Prime Minister,' writes David Walter. 'Something of an Oxford institution, [William] Rees-Mogg stood for election for office ten times in the Union; he was rejected for each of the four officers' chairs on separate occasions.' But he did eventually win the prize that always eluded Stanley Johnson: in his final term, he was elected Union president.[22]

Jacob tried to relive William's student days in precise detail. He told me:

> I joined the Union on the day I arrived at Oxford, taken in by my father, who gave me membership. I practically lived in the Oxford Union for three years. I joined OUCA within a few days of arriving. I was actually signed up by Simon Hoare [now a Tory MP], whom I just literally bumped into in the corridor [of the Commons] coming back to my office to take your call.

Rees-Mogg made his Union speaking debut with a eulogy to Thatcher's 'economic miracle'. Known for loudly rehearsing his speeches in his room, he would later recall 'Union debates in which I spoke frequently and prolixly, liking the sound of my own voice even if nobody else did', and 'putting rigorous Thatcherite arguments against woolly-minded liberals'.[23] He reflects now: 'Some of the routine oratorical tricks I probably picked up at Oxford – the obsession with everything coming in threes, that sort of thing.'

Almost immediately, *Cherwell* awarded him (as it had Gove in his first term) the traditional title of 'Pushy Fresher'.[24] Rees-Mogg, the paper reported, already had political networks that extended beyond the university: 'Jacob still returns to London on most of his free Tuesdays to lend a hand in the Conservative central office.' The article was illustrated by a photograph of Rees-Mogg speechifying in his suit, above the caption, 'What more need we say?'

Studying the picture of the eighteen-year-old dressed like a middle-aged upper-class man, you realise: three-plus decades later, Rees-Mogg is unchanged. Like Johnson and Gove, he has even kept the hairstyle of his Oxford days. When I asked him about his student outfit, he said, 'Funnily enough, I'm probably wearing exactly the same sort of suit sitting here talking to you now.'

The Tory public schoolboys arrived at Oxford almost fully formed. School had given them the confidence, articulacy and know-how to bestride the university. They had already constructed cartoon personal brands for themselves, which gave them instant recognition at Oxford.

They didn't spend university trying on new accents and personas; they already knew what they wanted to be when they grew up. They were climbing the greasy pole before most students had even located it.

Rees-Mogg made himself into possibly the biggest student celebrity since Johnson. 'I think there was a general sense that he was a great institution,'[25] recalled Dan Hannan. Rees-Mogg was the comic lord in outdated dress, heir to Lord Mauleverer of Greyfriars and the *Beano* magazine's Lord Snooty. 'English people are extremely fond of the titled ass', wrote Orwell, 'the seeming idiot who drawls and wears a monocle but is always to the fore in moments of danger'.[26]

Fiona Graham, the anthropologist of the Oxford Union, notes: 'In English ideology the eccentric is not on the outside of society criticising it, but is himself an integral part of society.' She says the eccentric is typically conformist in his beliefs, and eccentric only in 'external ways: mannerisms, clothes, speech, wit'.[27]

Rees-Mogg brought some assets to his campaign for the Union presidency in 1990: he was an entertaining British archetype who knew more famous people than just about any other student. He featured in *Cherwell* most weeks, albeit as a joke. But he says now: 'I'd have been much better off not being as forthright as I was about my Thatcherite views. That was not a great way to get elected.' In truth, the future minister for Brexit opportunities was probably just too peculiar to be put in charge of Oxford's biggest institution. He lost the election to the future Tory minister for security and borders, Damian Hinds. In 1991 Rees-Mogg did follow his father in becoming president of

OUCA, with *Cherwell* citing his 'campaign for world domination and social adequacy'.[28]

*

For anyone trying to explain the Oxford Tory Brexiteers, school is a big part of their story, but so is university. Rachel Johnson says, 'The Oxford networks are important, the Union is important, the pipeline into the Tory Party is important, the presence of other ambitious young men with very acute political antennae is also, because they could hone each other.'

If someone had polled undergraduates in the 1980s to guess who would be ruling Britain in the 2020s, I suspect most would have named Johnson, Gove and Rees-Mogg. Oliver Campbell, a Union president in 1991, adds: 'It was easier to predict that they would be influential than to predict what form that influence would take.'

This generation had ambition without a cause. I don't think they dreamed of making policy at Westminster. Ideology has rarely been a major driving force of the British ruling caste. Rosa Ehrenreich noted: 'The assumption at Oxford seemed to be that the world should be taken as it is. Class differences exist and can never be entirely over-ridden. Power differences exist.' Oxford's offer to ambitious students, she concluded, was that 'maybe someday you will be on top of the heap yourself'.[29]

This world-view – or lack of a conscious world-view – has sometimes benefited Britain. Ignorant and suspicious of philosophy, Oxford politicos instinctively mock the funny-sounding new-fangled utopian ideologies that have sometimes ensnared French or German elites. Marxism, with its strangled terminology, never stood a chance in Britain. Oxford in particular was too ironic for radicalism. Kingsley Amis, one of the few post-war undergraduates to join the university's branch of the Communist Party, explained later: 'At least ... it involved girls, not very nice looking ones, though.'[30] The British emphasis on witty, deflating rhetoric was itself a bulwark against dangerous ideas. George Steiner, the continental intellectual-turned-Cambridge don, diagnosed:

> If the Lord God came to England and started expound-ing his beliefs, you know what they'd say? They'd say, 'Oh, come off it!' Yes, this land is blessed with a powerful mediocrity of mind. It has saved you from communism and it has saved you from fascism. In the end you don't care enough about ideas to suffer their consequences.[31]

The Rees-Mogg brigade wanted to go to Westminster to make great British speeches, a mix of Churchill's 'blood, sweat and tears' and the witty repartee of Prime Minister's Question Time. They didn't particularly aspire to change Britain, or anybody's lives except their own.

8

UNION AND NON-UNION

*A happy island of pleasure finders and truth
seekers in the middle of the university. We were
always aware of the wrathful, contorted faces
of non-members lapping at the gates.*

Boris Johnson, recalling in 2002 how the Oxford
Union had been perceived in his day.[1]

At the start of the 1980s, the Union had been a small circle
of debating obsessives. But then it hit financial trouble,
and began recruiting among the broader student population.[2] By 1988, nearly half of Oxford's undergraduates had
paid the £65 joining fee.[3] But most of the new members
remained outsiders, on the grounds of class, gender or
political outlook. Their exclusion from this elite training
ground shapes British politics to this day.

The future Labour politician Andrew Adonis, son of a
Cypriot immigrant postman, had spent part of his upbringing in a council children's home. In his decade at Oxford
he recalls attending only one Union debate, for which the
motion was 'This House would abolish private schools'.
Adonis tried to speak in favour, but as he remembers it,

the president, William Hague, himself a comprehensive-school boy, only called on his private-school chums.

Adonis took his political energies elsewhere, and in 1987, almost uniquely among students of his era, got elected to Oxford city council. His campaign posters blanketed the city centre, piquing the interest of a Balliol classics student. Decades later, when Adonis was transport secretary, Johnson, the mayor of London, told him, 'I saw your posters everywhere, and I always wanted to meet the great and beautiful Adonis.'

The Union's costumes and debating rules – 'Point of order!' 'Point of information!' – were intimidatingly arcane to most students, but second nature to the public-school boys who had grown up with public speaking. It was as if it was a language that only they knew. Untrained outsiders who somehow got onstage risked getting eaten alive. Luntz reflects, 'I was so destroyed by the interventions, by the hostility of the chamber, that I started to read [his speeches]. So it killed my confidence. They were so much better than me. The words came to them easy. They didn't come to me easy. I thought I was a good debater and I learned that I wasn't.'

Foremost among the excluded in the Union of the 1980s were, still, women. The Union had admitted them as full members only in 1963, after forty years of pushing for entry;[4] Heath had spoken against their admission in 1938.[5]

The Union politico Zoe Johnson (no relation), reflecting in 1987 on why it remained so hard for women to rise in both the Union and the Commons, noted among many other reasons: 'It is harder for a woman to stand and debate in that august chamber. Soft, high-pitched voices fade into insignificance. Greater attention is paid to your appearance than to your speech.'[6]

Most women also lacked rhetorical training. When I asked Rachel Johnson whether she had been taught public speaking at her posh girls' schools, Bryanston and St Paul's, she replied:

No, Christ no! I think the only time I ever went to a debate at St Paul's was when I was asked to go back and give a class at St Paul's about giving speeches. Even St Paul's, the best girls' school in the country, couldn't offer a comparable experience. As a female you aren't encouraged to show off in the same way, and dazzle, and amuse – all those things that are so important. Because it's part of that killer quality that Theresa May never got, which is charm. If you can deploy charm, you're already winning.

And so the mass of students, even those who were political obsessives, tended just to shut up and watch Union debates, or stay away altogether. A small elite hogged the stage. One male lower-middle-class student, who was too frightened even to make a point of information during debates, told me: 'There was something glorious and fun about it. These people are fun, they are entertaining. You do get to jeer from the audience, and cheer for points of information. It's a circus. I didn't think, "These people are going to be prime minister."'

★

The 1980s' Left had excluded itself from the Union. Oxford's relatively small Labour Club had been boycotting the place since 1972, balking at the Union's entitled callowness and pricey joining fee. 'Retreating into their miserable dungareed caucuses', sneered Boris Johnson.[7]

There is a longstanding Labour tradition in the Oxford Union: Michael Foot became president in 1933 (though he was a Liberal at the time),[8] and three of his rival candidates for Labour leader in 1976 – Tony Benn, Tony Crosland and Roy Jenkins – had also been Union officers. Jenkins, looking back on his Union career decades later, admitted: 'In June 1940, I was almost as cast down by defeat for the presidency as by the fall of France.'[9] But the Union has never been as central to Labour as it is to the Tories. Clement Attlee, Hugh Gaitskell, Harold Wilson and Tony Blair didn't bother with the society while at Oxford; Attlee only used its library.[10] Blair honed his communication skills elsewhere – onstage, and in a rock band.

Even after the Labour Club ended its boycott in 1986,[11] few left-wingers embraced the Union. Daniel Hannan, in an article written for a student magazine in his last year at Oxford, pointed out that there wasn't much in it for them: 'It is a quirk of our party system that while an ambitious young Tory who succeeds in Oxford politics is well on the way towards a safe seat, an ambitious young socialist who offers himself for selection on the basis of a glittering Oxford career is likely to be met with a disinterested suggestion that he join a Trade Union.'

Nor did Oxford Labourites pay much attention to the plight of the working classes in the city where they lived. (Perhaps the Oxford working classes weren't desperate for students to join their struggle. Christopher Hitchens, who in the late 1960s joined the Oxford branch of 'the International Socialist *groupuscule*', recalled 'a demonstration, assiduously prepared for by mass factory-gate leafleting, to which exactly no workers showed up.')[12] The club took more interest in the national struggle, joining pickets for the miners' strike of 1984–85. It was a way for club members to meet real, live members of the working class – and striking miners were the ultimate fetish.

For the most part, ambitious Labourites tended to focus on policy that affected students' lives. Hannan mocked their concern 'with excruciatingly relevant *issues* – student loans, housing, or involvement with local government'. Dave Miliband chaired the accommodation committee of the Oxford University Student Union (OUSU, an entirely different institution from the Oxford Union). Yvette Cooper, Eddie Balls and Ted Miliband each became president of their college's junior common room (JCR) – in effect, a shop steward for undergraduates. All three led students in contentious rent negotiations with their colleges.

In 1985 Keir Starmer, who had taken an undergraduate law degree at Leeds, came to Oxford for two years to study for a bachelor of civil law – a rare case of a member of Britain's 'other ranks' using graduate school to join the Oxbridge elite. Starmer quickly became popular among the twenty or so regulars at Labour Club meetings. He was genuinely working class, charismatic, good-looking, quite left-wing, a football fan, a skilled Northern Soul dancer, and at twenty-three years old, relatively mature. He also joined a small group of far-left activists called Socialist Self-Management.[13]

Yet there was one formative political experience that he missed at Oxford. With hindsight, one of his contemporaries in the Labour Club told me, the boycott of the Union carried a cost: 'The thing about the Union was that you learned to speak.' Labour Club members never did learn. Adonis says that whereas the Tory political style of the 2020s features debating tricks 'straight out of the Oxford Union', Labour rhetoric 'is straight out of PPE seminars, tortured debates about post-Marxism'.

While Johnson was honing his jokes on the Union's presidential throne, the Labour Club's meetings were all about proposing or seconding bureaucratic or international motions: 'We resolve to give £10 to Brown Rice Week', or 'We resolve to support the campaign of the Palestine Liberation Organisation'. Balls recalls that at his first meeting of the Club, in 1985, 'the main item on the agenda was whether or not to include the hammer-and-sickle on the club's new banner'.[14]

The Labour Club was also simply not very mediagenic. Then as now, the Tories were a better story. Luke Harding, editor of *Cherwell* for a term in 1989, recalls: 'Right-wing politics in Oxford in that era was sexier. Left-wing politics was worthy but less alluring. We did write serious stuff [in *Cherwell*] but I think we were a bit bedazzled by the aristos and their social games and political machinations. We thought that by laughing at them we could reduce them.'

The Labour Club did hold occasional debates. In one, Starmer argued vehemently for the printers' strike at Rupert Murdoch's new plant at Wapping, against a more hesitant, centrist club faction around Dave Miliband and Stephen Twigg.[15] But the rules and procedures beloved of the Labour movement killed high-wire speechifying. Nor had most Labourites learned the art at school. The consequences remain visible to this day: Starmer is a forensic speaker, but a dull and unfunny one, with a nasal voice.

Only one figure in 1980s Oxford seems to have successfully straddled the Labour–Union divide: Simon Stevens, a comprehensive-school boy who was the son of a Baptist minister-cum-teacher. In 1986 he went on a Union debating trip to the US with Johnson and Luntz.[16] Stevens and Johnson were friends, and Johnson would recall in 2019,[17] possibly accurately, that Stevens had helped get him elected Union president. In 1987, Stevens himself won the presidency. In that role he mused about dropping the white-tie requirement, and loosening the Union's links with OUCA.[18] Had he pursued Labour politics all the way to Westminster, he might have become quite a force.

9

BIRTH OF BREXIT

*We firmly believe that a majority of European citizens
opposes the creation of a Federal European State.*

Patrick Robertson, Oxford history undergraduate
and founding secretary of the Bruges Group,
in its launch manifesto, 9 February 1989

Until the late 1980s Thatcher – like almost all Tories of the
period – remained a good European. The European Commission had given Britain the rebate she had demanded,
and she was working with the commission's president,
Jacques Delors, to create a European single market. In
1986, the UK signed the European Community's Single
European Act.

Europe rarely came up as a political issue in Oxford
at the time. The mainstream issues were Britain's deploy-
ment of nuclear weapons, the miners' strike, and apartheid
(many Tories weren't very anti). But in September 1988,
a fortnight before Rees-Mogg (and I) started at Oxford,
Thatcher gave her famous 'Bruges speech', in which she
warned against 'a European super-state exercising a new
dominance from Brussels'. She had realised, rather late

in the day, that the single market would be accompanied by closer political integration. There was growing talk on the continent of a single currency. Now she turned Eurosceptic.

Her speech spooked the Oxford Tories. Ruling Britain was the prerogative of their caste. They didn't want outsiders in Brussels muscling in. Tory 'Euroscepticism' began in part as a jobs protection scheme, much like taxi drivers fighting back against Uber. And to some degree, Oxford public-school boys had come to think of the country they ruled as their own caste writ large. Nobody told Britain – even post-war Britain – what to do.

One Eurosceptic convert was Patrick Robertson, then a second-year history student at Oxford, a Scot who had grown up in Paris and Rome, where his leftist anti-Thatcher father worked for the British Tourist Authority.[1] In childhood, Robertson recalled, he and his brother used to 'visit England in September and go to Kew Gardens, buy our school uniform at Selfridges, and watch the last night of the Proms on television, enraptured by the atmosphere of an alien Britishness'. He told me, 'If you are brought up abroad, you have more of an affection and understanding of the qualities that British democracy is based on than many of the people who live here.'

Robertson decided, aged twelve, that he wanted to become an MP.[2] He boarded for a while at Dulwich College, flirted with Marxism, and came to see Britain as a country 'that needs preserving'. At Oxford, he became a minor Union hack. At a Burns Night Supper in 1988, the Union's then president Michael Gove kindly sat him next to a fellow Scot, Norman Stone. Robertson and Stone danced

Highland flings, got drunk,[3] and hit it off, especially when they discovered they were both Eurosceptics who spoke fluent Italian – in Stone's case, entirely self-taught.

When Thatcher gave her Bruges speech, Robertson didn't notice. It didn't get much play in the newspapers, he recalls, and anyway, he was busy writing his own anti-federalist screed. Only late in 1988 did he discover that the prime minister was on the same page. So were several other senior Conservatives. He began to contact them. *Cherwell* named him 'Pushy Fresher', mocking him as a fantasist for having sent a note inviting the visiting Edward Heath to meet him in the Crypt wine bar.[4]

In fact, though, Robertson was getting somewhere. He began shuttling back and forth to London to meet Eurosceptic powerbrokers. Thatcher admired him; he observed that she smelt like his mother.[5] He attended a dinner at the home of Christopher Monckton, a former member of her policy unit, where the idea of a referendum on Europe was discussed.[6] *Cherwell* grew fascinated with Robertson. In February 1989, it reported that the 'rather middle aged lady' who 'had started living with him and his girlfriend ... is in fact his secretary, hired on behalf of Paddy's Bruges Group, a decidedly dodgy organisation he's just set up to promote right wing economic views'.[7]

Soon afterwards, at the age of twenty, Robertson abandoned his degree and left Oxford to devote himself full time to his new think tank.[8] 'Much as I like European countries,' he explained, 'it's just wrong for Britain to be governed from an authority other than Westminster.'[9] At the time, wrote the Eurosceptic MP Bill Cash, the Bruges Group was 'the only organised opposition' to the EEC.[10]

Stone, whose photograph adorned Robertson's office,[11] became one of the group's intellectual godfathers.[12] Within months the organisation had attracted more than a hundred backbench MPs.[13] Its original aim, says Robertson, was to 'reform' Europe. Hardly anybody in those days could imagine leaving.

Today Robertson runs the public-relations firm WorldPR, lives in St Moritz, Switzerland, and is Kazakhstan's honorary consul to the Bahamas. He has remained a Thatcherite: in 2011 he spent £100 on flowers for the ex-prime minister, according to his offshore financial records. Besides Kazakhstan, WorldPR's clients have included Augusto Pinochet and autocratic Azerbaijan, while the firm also ran a post-Brexit 'Global Britain' campaign.[14]

But for all Robertson's early efforts, Oxford Euroscepticism was initially quite a marginal movement. Europe seemed awfully far away. On the night of 9 November 1989, I was having an essay crisis in my room when a friend banged at the door. 'What?' I shouted irritably. He yelled back: 'The Berlin Wall has fallen!' I was twenty years old, studying history and German, and this was the most inspiring political event of my lifetime. (It still is.) I stayed up all night imbibing the radio news.

The next afternoon, desperate to discuss these world-changing events with everybody else, I went to Junior Common Room tea. I pushed open the door of the JCR, and looked around in astonishment: nothing had changed. Just like every other day, people were reading the sports pages, gossiping and watching *Neighbours*. I thought for a second that they were playing a collective practical joke, and that in a moment they would all switch to debating the repercussions for the pro-democratic protests in Prague.

On Cornmarket that Saturday I saw a student selling the communist newspaper *The Morning Star*. 'Have you heard the news?' I asked. 'Now more than ever, mate!' he replied.

The next week, a friend and I went to a packed lecture on 'Marxist literary theory' by the literature don Terry Eagleton. His opening sentence was, 'The only thing that recent events in eastern Europe prove is that Marxism doesn't work when applied to underdeveloped countries.' 'Underdeveloped countries like East Germany and Czechoslovakia?' whispered my friend. The rest of the lecture was a paean to Marxism, during which the student to my right took elaborate notes. Peeking over his shoulder to see what he could possibly find worth writing down, I read his summary: 'Presumably ironic.'

It was quite a winter. Communism fell, and on 11 February 1990, Nelson Mandela walked out of prison. But I kept failing to grasp how faintly these distant events registered in Oxford. One day at *Cherwell*, a press invitation arrived for a 'luncheon talk' at OUCA by Geoffrey Howe, the deputy prime minister and recent foreign secretary. I was thrilled: this man at the centre of these earth-shattering events would be able to give us the inside story. I went expecting to find a packed hall. I came away baffled: why had Howe bothered to come? Why was nobody there, except me and a dozen Tory boys in suits? And why had nobody asked him about eastern Europe? I can't now remember a word he said.

A Hungarian master's student who had arrived at

Pembroke College that autumn also concluded that Oxford was not the place to experience the revolutions. Viktor Orbán broke off his studies to return home and stand in Hungary's general election of March 1990. About the only trace that Oxford seems to have left on him is a line in his official CV: 'In 1989–1990, Mr Orbán studied the history of British liberal political philosophy in Pembroke College, Oxford, sponsored by the Soros Foundation.'[15]

But during 1990, as the continent began to remake itself, Europe finally did become an issue at Oxford. What happened at the university then would end up casting its shadow all the way to 2016. For possibly the first time ever, Oxford began to hatch a revolution: Brexit.

The fall of the Berlin Wall had changed Europe. France and Germany soon agreed that the EEC would have to become more of a federal union, with a shared foreign policy and a common currency. The member-states began sketching out what would become the federalist Maastricht treaty. Meanwhile, the Conservatives defenestrated Thatcher in November 1990 just as her warning about a superstate seemed to be coming true. Three weeks later her successor, John Major, approved the Maastricht treaty's outlines.

Dan Hannan, then a Thatcherite history student in his first term at Oxford, spent these last weeks of the year in a state of outrage. He believed that the Tories had dumped his heroine in part because she opposed the single currency.

Like Patrick Robertson of the Bruges Group, Hannan had grown up worshipping Britain from afar – in his case, from his father's large poultry farm in Peru. The family had moved to Latin America from Lancashire after the

First World War,[16] but the men continued to import British wives and to frequent high-ceilinged clubs in Lima. Hannan grew up mentally inhabiting a Britain that no longer existed.

One of his earliest Peruvian memories was of his frail, elderly father confronting a mob that was trying to seize their estate.[17] Hannan told me over Zoom in 2021 that he spent his childhood 'in a country where politics didn't work and where there were repeated breakdowns, and where civil order was contingent and where constitutions were dreamed up regularly'. This was very unlike the experience of most 1980s Oxford politicos, who had grown up in the safest region in the safest period in history. Hannan's Peruvian experiences taught him to revere unchanging British institutions. By the age of nineteen he had already attended two: Marlborough College and Oxford.

He says:

Coming from Peru, I'd come from a place where people took politics quite seriously because the consequences were nasty if you got it wrong. And I'd never really, until Oxford, come across this idea of 'It's a hobby, just something that you're interested in and it's gossipy.' I was thinking, 'Who are all these people who are treating this as an automatic leg-up into Parliament, and why? What are they doing it for? What's the point of going into elected politics without a strong agenda?' I thought, 'The only thing that really matters is: Are you doing this out of high principle?'

One other thing distinguished Hannan from his fellow

Oxford politicos: despite his British nationalism, he had an international world-view. When the Maastricht treaty came along, he took it seriously. He didn't assume that democracy would inevitably survive, and he scrutinised the upheavals in eastern Europe.

There was a period of about three years in the early '90s when [Maastricht] led the news every day in the way the coronavirus is leading the news now.

I'd spent part of my gap year in what we then still called Eastern Europe, watching the unfolding revolutions. In fact, in most of the places I'd been, it was that period at the start of 1990 when free elections had been scheduled but not yet held. So the Communists were still in power, but everyone could see the change was coming, except them, weirdly. I remember this extraordinary conversation with a Hungarian apparatchik explaining to me how they would win the election, and how the so-called democratic opposition only had their marijuana and their Pink Floyd albums, and people like me fell for them because they spoke good English.

Having seen that and having been quite impressed by the 'people power' of restoring national democracy, this Maastricht thing came as quite a bolt from the blue. For me in 1990 it was very clear that the primary motive force for the democratic revolutions in Czechoslovakia, Poland, Rumania or whatever was ending the foreign occupation of their country.

There was a moment that really woke me up when the Latvian foreign minister was doing a visit to the

UK. It was that time when the Baltic states were the first to leave the USSR, and the foreign minister was asked some question about, 'Are you really independent? You haven't printed your own currency yet,' and all this. And he said, 'Well, we're more independent than the United Kingdom.'

And I remember thinking, 'Gosh, actually, that's technically true, isn't it? They have complete jurisdiction, complete sovereignty, there's no foreign court that can overrule their statutes. How extraordinary that this tiny little country that had one blip of existence before has managed to achieve this sovereignty. When did we ever discuss giving ours up? When was that ever agreed?' So that was the context in which Maastricht came. And that was and has remained my primary objection to it: that it was incompatible with democratic self-government.

As an articulate public schoolboy, Hannan in his first term had already become a presence in Oxford's political circles. Once the new treaty became an issue, he says,

I remember going around and having a few conversations with people. It takes quite an effort of will at this distance to recall what a surprise all this was, how shocking it was that, 'Hang on, suddenly it's being presented that we're going to be a sort of province in a bigger entity called Europe with its own flag and anthem and passport and everything.' I was struck by how many people shared my distrust of what was going on. And I began to think, 'This is urgent'.

His co-conspirators were his Marlborough schoolfriend Mark Reckless, who would go on to become a Tory and then a UKIP MP, and James Ross, a musician who had briefly lived in Hungary after communism and is now a conductor.[18] In December 1990, the three of them met either at the seventeenth-century Queens Lane Coffee House on the High Street, or at the thirteenth-century Bear Inn (there is some disagreement as to the venue) and founded the Oxford Campaign for an Independent Britain.

With hindsight, the CIB – which would intertwine with the Bruges Group – looks like the genesis of the campaign for Brexit. Owen Matthews, who became its social secretary because he was good at organising cocktail parties, calls the group 'the Ur-Brexit gang'. He compares the CIB's founders to the early Bolsheviks. Hannan in 1990 was Marx in 1848: the man who sketched the paradise to come. He would become arguably the most influential theorist of Brexit, and therefore the most influential British political thinker since Thatcher. Rees-Mogg recalls, 'I think he thought it [leaving the EU] through to its logical conclusion long before I did.'

Matthews says that the CIB 'had the glamour of being a somewhat upstart, purist, fundamentalist movement'.

Dan was the voice crying in the wilderness long before Brexit became mainstream or fashionable in the Conservative Party. The more serious part of the CIB was Hayekian set-Britain-free libertarianism. Hannan helped move Euroscepticism from a fringe of loony 'bastards' to an intellectually respectable minority in the Tory party of sufficient weight to push Cameron into backing the referendum.

David Allen Green, a Eurosceptic student from Birmingham who later became a lawyer and a commentator on Brexit, recalls: 'Hannan was a polite and pleasant person. I thought he was the one person who was really on top of the materials. He had actually read the Maastricht treaty, and would quote from it. He was also highly regarded as a historian. Everyone knew he had got a First in Mods [the first-year exams].'

During Hannan's later years as a Conservative MEP in Brussels, a committee photo of the CIB would hang on his wall.[19] Among the dozen bright-eyed students gazing confidently into the future with him are Sara Maynard, who became his wife, and Roger Bird, who became (briefly) general secretary of UKIP.

The CIB tended to attract Oxford's posher, dining-club Tories, albeit that few were as posh as Hannan himself. One of the CIB's first members was Jacob Rees-Mogg,[20] though he recalls having been more preoccupied with his looming Finals: 'I think that is the one point in my Oxford career where I may have been concentrating on History.' Most other ambitious student Tories of the day – George Osborne, Rory Stewart (who had been in the same house as Rees-Mogg at Eton) and Nicky Griffith (later Nicky Morgan, Gove's successor as education secretary in 2014) – steered clear. 'They thought it was a little too outré and insurgent, not career-enhancing,' says Matthews.

Hannan admits that the CIB might have included some nostalgic Little Englander types: 'There's a kind of person who goes through a bit of a young fogey phase when they leave home for the first time.' But in his memory, the CIB represented an unspoiled Euroscepticism before the advent of loud-mouthed xenophobes who would put off future generations of students.

Within a term at Oxford, says Hannan, 'We had I think over 300 members. I think we peaked at slightly more than that in the end. They were by no means all right of centre. Probably the majority, but not overwhelmingly. You can't be the second biggest political society on campus without having a broad diversity of people.'

Cherwell began to pay the CIB the compliment of frequent mockery: 'What is such a group of people, harbouring huge grudges against everything and anything from across the Channel, doing spending so much time in a restaurant devoted to Italian cuisine?'[21] The CIB's issues quickly went mainstream. In November 1991 the Oxford Union invited Heath and Norman Tebbit to debate the motion, 'The proposed European Union offers little of value to the United Kingdom'. The evening opened with the unveiling of the bust of Heath that still stands in the Union chamber. The man himself told the chamber: 'Fifty-five years ago when I first sat on these benches I never imagined that a bust would appear ... nor did I imagine for a moment that I would be addressing this society in duplicate.' But then what would prove to be a premonitory internal Tory quarrel over Europe broke out. Heath was hissed for repeatedly refusing to give way on points of information. The anti-European motion passed by 108 votes.[22]

In 1992 Hannan became OUCA president, defeating

Nicky Griffith. But he wasn't a Brexiteer yet at Oxford. Nor were most CIBers. The very concept of leaving the EEC was a fringe, almost crackpot idea in the early 1990s. Hannan at the time wanted the UK to strike an associate deal with the EEC, telling the Europeans, in effect, 'Look, you guys go ahead with unified foreign policy, criminal justice, etcetera. We wish you well, but we're just going to stick with the market bit.'

Meanwhile, a rebel group of like-minded Tory anti-Maastricht MPs had emerged in parliament, led by figures such as Bill Cash (an Oxford history graduate of an earlier generation) and Nicholas Ridley. Hannan says:

> I'd met most of these guys as an undergraduate. I saw they were under an immense amount of pressure from the party establishment, and anything that I could do as a student just to make them feel a bit more supported and to remind them that there was a lot of public sympathy for their position was worth doing. So we had most of them to come and speak at Oxford.

The Maastricht rebels would also speak at the Union and OUCA or the University's Bruges Group. Matthews says,

> They talked to us as though naturally expecting us to take up the torch at a national political level. In other words, the Godfathers of Brexit were personally familiar interlocutors for politically active students at Oxford. Which of course made the transition to parliament and the Cabinet much more of a natural

progression for the whole cohort. The Dan Hannans
of this world were anointed early.

They lost their first battle: in February 1992, Major signed
the Maastricht treaty, though he opted out of the single
currency and the 'Social Chapter'. William Rees-Mogg's
court challenge to Maastricht – he called it the most
important constitutional case in 300 years – was defeated.[23]

But it was a time of intellectual ferment. A Eurosceptic
ecosystem was emerging. Robertson told me: 'Margaret
Thatcher resigns, and literally the first thing she does [in
January 1991] is become president of the Bruges Group.
That was considered a quite significant thing. Nigel Farage
told me it had quite an impact on him, too.' Also in 1991,
Alan Sked, who was then head of European studies at the
London School of Economics, founded the Anti-Federalist
League, which would soon become the UK Independ-
ence Party, or UKIP.[24] The movement had emerged at the
right time. With the trade unions and the Soviet Union
defeated, the British right needed a new enemy. The EU
was the obvious candidate.

Eurosceptics at Oxford were genuinely trying to work
out what kind of Europe they wanted. And many different options still seemed open. 'The outcome of this push
towards federalism was, at the time, uncertain,' says David
Allen Green. In June 1992, thrillingly, the Danes rejected
Maastricht in a referendum. That September, on 'Black
Wednesday', the European Exchange Rate Mechanism
collapsed. Both events seemed to validate the Oxford
Eurosceptics. Green says, 'This is so important: people
genuinely thought they could defeat the Maastricht treaty.

For a lot of people, the critique of the Maastricht treaty was the entry drug into Brexit.'

Oxford's pro- and anti-European students held many of their debates in the Union – not so much in the Chamber itself, but in smaller venues like the Library or the Morris Room. There were impromptu late-night arguments in the bar. Green also recalls somebody kidnapping the bust of the pro-European Heath – 'very much the bogey' – from the Chamber.

In July 1993, the Maastricht treaty received royal assent. Hannan, who had just graduated, says he experienced the moment 'as an immense defeat', and was left thinking:

> 'Where does it go from here? We've lost, the treaty's in place, we're not going to be able to undo it, at least not in the short term, so how does Euroscepticism reinvent itself? We need to have a much wider critique of what's wrong with the centralisation of power. We need to put it in terms that everyone can relate to and we need to find like-minded allies on the continent.'
>
> I thought, 'I'm not prepared to drop this thing, it's too important. And I know a lot of the players and let's see if we can't turn things around.'
>
> So I wrote to a number of the MPs who had come to speak to the CIB and said, 'This is what I think we ought to be doing,' and a number of them wrote back and said, 'Wonderful, I couldn't agree more.'

He then returned to the rebel MPs with a suggestion: '"What if you all clubbed together, you can employ me, your share of my salary would be only this" – the only enterprising thing I've ever done in terms of my salary. And they said yes.'

At twenty-one years old, Hannan became a full-time Brexiteer.[25] He had attached his political ambitions not to a party but to an ideal. While almost everyone else in politics was watching the news cycle, he kept his eyes on a bigger prize. He helped the rebel MP Michael Spicer create a parliamentary movement of a couple of dozen anti-Maastricht MPs, called the European Research Group (ERG). 'I was the first secretary, first employee,' Hannan recalls.

> I was involved for four or five years, and in those days it was still doing a lot of research. Perhaps the name was deliberately chosen to be unthreatening, but it was not bogus. I mean, we were producing many papers on what was wrong with the Common Agricultural Policy, what was wrong with the Common Fisheries Policy, the euro, what would be our blueprint for a better kind of EU that we could live with, all this kind of thing. It was mainly me, but I was doing some farming out of that stuff to other people.

The Eurosceptic ecosystem grew. In 1994 Robertson helped sell the idea of a referendum on the nature of Britain's EU membership to Sir James Goldsmith, who founded the Referendum Party;[26] the twenty-three-year old Priti Patel became its press officer.

Future elites were getting involved in Hannan's fight, both for and against. In 1992, the pro-federalist Oxford Reform Club was created as a rival to the CIB. By 1995, the club's president, the PPEist Ollie Robbins, was inviting students to 'star attractions', such as a talk on the euro by the German embassy's finance attaché, and an event called 'selling Europe to the citizen'. In 2017, Robbins would become Theresa May's chief negotiator with the EU on Brexit.[27]

By 1997, the seventeen-year-old editor of the Winchester College newspaper, Rishi Sunak, soon to go up to Oxford, was fretting that Tony Blair 'has plans for the possible break-up of the United Kingdom and membership of an eventual European Superstate'.[28] In 1998, twenty-six-year-old Dominic Cummings became campaign director of Business for Sterling, a group that opposed Blair's plans to join the euro.[29] Hannan's struggle had found its master communicator.

10

A GENERATION
WITHOUT TRAGEDY

Have in honour you who enter here
All those sons of this house
Who went forth to serve in the years
1914–1918
War memorial in Magdalen College, Oxford

There is something eternal about the Johnson–Cameron–
Hannan generation: a group of well-spoken young men
saunter from public school through Oxford to power,
armoured by the certainty that nothing very bad can
ever happen to their caste. Versions of these men recur
throughout modern British history.

Popular frustration with them is old, too. Even by the
1850s, the disasters of the Crimean War and the Indian
Mutiny had discredited the gentleman amateur. The historian Richard Colls writes of Crimea:

It was not just that the Duke of Cambridge, 35 years
old and in charge of the First Infantry Division, was

the Queen's cousin, or that Estcourt, the Adjudant General, most unfortunately had his photograph taken sleeping in a deckchair in the middle of the gravest crisis in British military history, or that Lord Raglan the Commander-in-Chief had last seen active service against Napoleon, or that Lords Cardigan and Lucan all but destroyed the cavalry between them.[1]

In a Victorian proto-version of chumocracy, Raglan employed four relatives as aides-de-camp.[2] Though the catastrophic Charge of the Light Brigade was spun at home as a glorious imperial romp,[3] the Crimean debacles prompted reforms of the army and civil service. Even so, the amateur ruler, lightly seasoned by Oxbridge tutorials, persisted in British history. Read, for instance, the critique by Lord Curzon (Eton and Oxford, where he was president of the Union) of Arthur Balfour (Eton and Cambridge), Britain's foreign secretary after 1916. Curzon describes

the lamentable ignorance, indifference and levity of [Balfour's] regime. He never studied his papers, he never knew the facts, at the Cabinet he had seldom read the morning's Foreign Office telegrams, and he never looked ahead. He trusted to his unequalled powers of improvisation to take him through any trouble and enable him to leap lightly from one crisis to another.[4]

Curzon (chancellor of Oxford University when he wrote this, and Balfour's future successor as foreign secretary) is also, of course, describing Boris Johnson.

Yet there is a crucial difference between Balfour's era and Johnson's: a century ago, British politicians took their jobs more seriously. After all, they were governing about a quarter of the world. One of the side effects of ruling colonies was that public schoolboys acquired administrative experience, often through trial and terrible error: Curzon, as Viceroy of India, had overseen the deaths of over a million Indians in the famine of 1899–1900. At home, Victorian Oxford public schoolboys learned from running powerful local governments. And they took wars especially seriously because they sent their sons to fight in them.

In June 1914, the CV of the twenty-year-old Harold Macmillan looked a lot like that of the future twenty-year-old Boris Johnson: an upper-middle-class upbringing, Eton, classics at Balliol College, and election as librarian of the Oxford Union by two votes.[5] Macmillan was a callow youth without a mission, who had grown up in isolation from the mass of the population. Had the peace held and he had gone on to serve his term as librarian, he might have stayed that way.

But in the summer of 1914, his CV and Johnson's diverged: 'At the end of July, instead of going off on a reading party to start reading for Greats, I found myself on a barrack square.'[6] He joined up as a second lieutenant in a new rifle battalion that didn't yet have any rifles.[7] Public schoolboys of his generation had been raised on stories of battlefield glory, albeit without machine guns. Joining up – typically as junior officers – was what they did. Meanwhile, the Oxford Union was converted into an officers' mess.[8]

Macmillan was seriously wounded three times in the war.[9] Once, after being hit in the knee and pelvis, he lay in a shell hole for twelve hours, medicating himself with morphine, playing dead when Germans came near, and reading Aeschylus in the original Greek.[10] Yet in 1916 he refused his anxious mother's suggestion that he apply for a safe staff job.[11]

Seven Union presidents died in the First World War, including three of the four who had held the post between the summers of 1912 and 1913.[12] This was part of a broader class sacrifice. 'At a time when the undergraduate population never exceeded 3,000, nearly 2,700 members of the University were killed in that war,' marvelled Jan Morris.[13] 'British losses were highest among junior officers', notes Colls.[14] 'Bertie Wooster, if he ever existed, was killed round about 1915', wrote Orwell.[15]

Macmillan did not return to Oxford after the war. 'It was not just that I was still a cripple', he explained later. 'There were plenty of cripples. But I could not face it. To me it was a city of ghosts. Of our eight scholars and exhibitioners [at Balliol] who came up in 1912, Humphrey Sumner and I alone were alive. It was too much.'[16]

Decades later, Macmillan reflected that upper-class officers such as himself, leading working-class troops, 'learnt for the first time how to ... feel at home with a whole class with whom we could not have come into contact in any other way'. It was in the trenches, and later in his north-eastern parliamentary constituency of Stockton-on-Tees, that Macmillan absorbed 'the duty to mitigate, as far as possible, the injustices suffered by the less privileged – be they Guardsmen, Durham miners or Stockton steelworkers', writes his biographer Charles Williams.[17]

In the British tradition, an upper-class junior officer

was responsible for his soldiers' lives. It was a paternalistic yet deeply responsible relationship. No wonder Macmillan could never afterwards shake the 'inside feeling that something awful and unknown was about to happen'. Ever since 1914, he said nearly seventy years later, 'the sky has been overcast and still is'.[18]

From 1940 to 1963, Britain was ruled by prime ministers who had volunteered for the front in the First World War.[19] Churchill, having been ousted from government after Gallipoli, got himself appointed commander of a battalion of the Royal Scots Fusiliers in 1916, aged forty-one. He was nearly killed on the Belgian front.

Clement Attlee fought at Gallipoli, where he was one of the last men out of the Suvla sector. He was wounded in Mesopotamia – hit by shrapnel while running ahead of his troops during an attack on Turkish lines – and later again in France.[20]

Anthony Eden won a Military Cross for carrying back a wounded sergeant from no-man's land under German fire.[21] Two of his three brothers died in the war,[22] as did a third of his class from Eton. When the surviving Oxford men went into politics, they were known by their wartime ranks: Major Attlee, Major Eden, Captain Macmillan.[23]

Three more Union presidents fell in the Second World War.[24] Another, Heath, participated in the Normandy landings, was mentioned in dispatches,[25] and was awarded an MBE aged twenty-nine. He said later that seeing Europe destroy itself again left him 'with the deep belief that remains with me to this day: that the peoples of Europe must never again be allowed to fight each other.'[26] In 1973 he took the UK into the EEC.

James Callaghan, a lieutenant in the East Indies fleet,[27] was the last British prime minister who served in combat. 'I cannot claim an heroic experience of war,' he later wrote. 'However, I saw enough on the lower deck and in the wardroom to know what the Navy expected when the war was won and men and women came back to Britain after four or five years abroad.' It surely isn't a coincidence that the era of war-veteran prime ministers was also the era of British social democracy. Both eras ended simultaneously, with Callaghan's defeat to Thatcher in 1979.

Eton is covered in plaques and monuments to masters and old boys killed in war. 'We all live in the shadows of the dead', felt the future writer and Tory operative Ferdinand Mount when he was a pupil there in the 1950s. 'The whole place is one huge chantry for departed souls.'[28] So was Oxford. One of my strongest memories of the place is the 'For King and Country' plaques that hang in all the colleges. 'The lists of the dead in the war memorials at Christ Church [College] include two viscounts, three earls, seven lords by courtesy, four baronets, eleven honourables, an Italian marquis and a French count', wrote Jan Morris. The one at New College includes old boys who died for Germany in the First World War.[29]

The upper class would remain marked for decades by its caste sacrifice. One evening in the mid 1990s I went to dinner (boarding-school stodge) at the House of Lords with Lord Lyell (Eton and Oxford). On the way to the dining room he pointed out the memorial to peers who had fallen in the First World War. The Lyell on that board was his grandfather. Then he pointed out the memorial to the dead of the Second World War: that Lyell was his father.

I don't want to idealise soldiers. Experience of war doesn't always forge nobility of soul. However, world wars are the most efficient means that the modern UK has found to throw the classes together. The closest Britain has ever got to One Nation may have been in the trenches, even if the officers slept in beds and the men on the ground.[30] Charles Ryder in *Brideshead* discerns this same melting of classes in the Second World War, much as he abhors it. Oxford men of the 1950s still got a shimmer of this experience from National Service (though Michael Heseltine escaped his just nine months into the requisite two years, freed to contest a hopeless seat for the Tories).[31]

From the 1940s until the 1970s, most senior British politicians were Oxbridge men who had fought in a world war. Joint wartime service created a sense of unity among leaders of rival parties: it felt natural to Attlee to join his fellow veterans Eden and Churchill in the coalition cabinet of 1940–45.

And fighting in wars helped turn these men into serious rulers. They had learned that decisions taken by Etonians in military HQ or behind Whitehall desks could kill people. That seriousness helps explain why, in the fifty years after the Second World War, British politicians largely avoided disaster, with the brief exception of Suez.

But the last MPs who were veterans of a world war – Heath, Tony Benn, Peter Emery and Geoffrey Johnson Smith – left parliament in 2001.[32] Then Bertie Wooster rose from the dead.

★

By the 1950s, hardly any British undergraduates had experience of combat. Foreign students who came to Oxford in the grip of their own wars inevitably found the natives callow. One such native, Christopher Hitchens, recalled with awe American students of the late 1960s huddled in 'tight little circles on the lawn as the Oxford dusk came on: should they defy the draft and become outlaws, with the choice of prison or exile, or submit and become obedient and get on with their careers?'[33]

At the end of the 1960s, the American Rhodes Scholars Strobe Talbott, Frank Aller and Bill Clinton were sharing a house at 46 Leckford Road in north Oxford. Talbott says the three of them spent their time conducting a 'permanent, floating, teacherless seminar on Vietnam'. He remembers one Thanksgiving when his two roommates discussed the war for four hours straight in the kitchen while basting the turkey.

Clinton spent much of his time at Oxford reading. He later calculated he had got through 300 books in his first year.[34] Classified I-A, meaning, 'Available for combat service', he was mentally readying himself to be sent to Vietnam. After hearing of former high-school classmates who had been killed in the war, he was wrestling with giving up his draft deferment. Two other Rhodes Scholars recall that he didn't even bother renting a flat in Oxford in autumn 1969, sleeping on people's floors instead.[35]

But then Clinton got lucky. The authorities decided to select the young men who would be called up by holding a lottery of their birthdates. When the lottery was conducted on 1 December 1969, the number assigned to Clinton's birthday was so high as to make it virtually certain that he wouldn't be drafted. Aller was unluckier: he resisted the draft, and was indicted in absentia by a Federal grand jury in Spokane, Washington. In 1971, aged twenty-four, he committed suicide.[36]

Talbott wrote to me: 'Vietnam was the big dark cloud over our heads. Frank was a tragedy of that. I don't recall that any of us thought much about the UK ruling class.'[37] Martin Walker writes in his biography of Clinton that the future president 'took almost no part in the Oxford Union'.[38]

This wasn't only because of Vietnam. The Rhodes Scholars, writes Walker, 'recalled snooty undergraduates, languid dons, cold rooms, and bad food. From the vantage point of an elite enclave, they experienced Britain as a country in palpable decline.' These men were the future ruling elite of a superpower. Like American Rhodies before and since, they had come to Oxford to network with each other, not with teenaged Brits. The plan worked: Rhodes Scholars like Talbott and Robert Reich ended up running the world with Clinton.

British unseriousness climaxed twenty years later in the Cameron/Johnson generation. These men had no personal experience of tragedy. They were the most privileged members of the luckiest generation of a country that for 300 years had avoided revolution, dictatorship, famine, civil war, invasion or economic meltdown. Tragedies did happen in Ireland and the empire, but only as offstage noises that scarcely registered with the ruling caste. The caste's own ancestral family tragedies – the dead of two world wars – had been recast, with the passing of time, as glories.

Some members of this public-school generation actively craved tragedy. They longed for their own heroic project. But Hannan aside, it took them a few decades to think of one.

11

ADULTS NOW

*The classic [British] route to fame and fortune, from public
school to university to the Bar to the House of Commons,
has involved moving through ancient institutions without
ever having to hire, fire or manage other people ... The time-
honoured Oxbridge structures – on top of the foundations
of medieval schools – can easily encourage their inhabitants
towards the most conventional kind of ambition, to
climb up existing trees rather than plant new ones...*

Anthony Sampson, *The Changing Anatomy of Britain*[1]

And then one day my Oxford years were suddenly over.
My departure was smoother than Macmillan's. In July 1992
my father drove up from London and parked outside the
Radcliffe Camera. We shoved my bags into the boot and
motored out of town. It felt like ten minutes since the
afternoon in October 1988 when he'd parked outside the
Radcliffe Camera and I'd run into college to ask the porter
for my room key.

Most of the people I had known at Oxford went on to
groom the lower slopes of the establishment as civil servants, academics, fundraisers and solicitors. Thirty years

on, they have comfortable middle-class existences, living in the provinces and worrying about their mortgages. They have followed the Oxford track for people without particular connections or ambitions.

I'd had a wonderful time at Oxford, but I left feeling both psychologically and intellectually unprepared for adulthood. I was painfully aware that I had been undereducated. In the Netherlands, where I had grown up, pupils sitting the final high-school exams aged eighteen did seven or eight subjects. In Britain, I'd sat four A-levels, meaning that my knowledge of all other academic fields was adolescent at best. As Rosa Ehrenreich notes: 'Oxford produces scientists who haven't read a work of literature since they were fifteen, language students who know nothing of history, law students who know nothing of politics.'[2]

The classic British three-year undergraduate degree is one of the shortest in the western world as it is, but my time at Oxford had amounted to just seventy-two term-time weeks, or a bit under a year and a half of actual work, when I wasn't drinking with other wasters in the college bar. I'd also spent a fascinating year living in Berlin just after the Wall fell, studying at the city's Technical University. My degree had given me a smattering of history, and a narrow knowledge of German literature. I knew little about any other subject, and almost nothing about the sciences. Nor did I fully understand what interest rates were, let alone why they went up and down. Looking back, I shared the frustration later expressed by Dominic Cummings about the limits of an undergraduate arts degree:

If you want to figure out what characters around

Putin might do, or how international criminal gangs might exploit holes in our border security, you don't want more Oxbridge English graduates who chat about [French psychoanalyst Jacques] Lacan at dinner parties with TV producers and spread fake news about fake news.[3]

Like Cummings, but less ferociously, I decided that the remedy for this ignorance was lifelong learning. He was encouraged by Norman Stone to go to post-communist Russia, where he became a failed entrepreneur, setting up an airline between Samara and Vienna that once took off forgetting its only passenger.[4] Afterwards he plunged into autodidactic study. I took an institutional route: I went to Harvard to study economics, politics and Russian for a year, and ended up delving into mysteries I had never previously contemplated, such as how exchange rates worked.

The combined workload for the various classes at Harvard was much bigger than at Oxford – total reading assignments alone routinely exceeded 1,000 pages a week – yet I rarely experienced a conversational prompt to thought. On the other hand, I hadn't very often at Oxford either, mostly because I hadn't put in the work.

Cambridge, Massachusetts, was a popular destination for the more wonkish Oxford politicos. David Miliband, Ed Balls, Yvette Cooper and the future Tory thinker Nick Boles were all Kennedy Scholars at Harvard in the late 1980s and early 1990s. Ed Miliband later took a sabbatical there too. These people tended to gravitate around the Kennedy School, Harvard's school of government. The brick-and-glass edifice on the Charles River is a home for mostly centre-left wonks, a place where the cafeteria echoes with squeals of excitement over a promising policy experiment in Kentucky kindergartens.

Also running around Harvard at the time was Fiona Hill, who, after being rejected by Oxford, had ended up with a PhD in Russian history. Harvard eventually channelled her into Washington's foreign-policy establishment. She said her poor origins and 'very distinctive working-class accent' never impeded her career in America as they would have in Britain.[5] In fact, most Americans couldn't even identify her as working class. Tellingly, the right-wing radio host Rush Limbaugh misidentified her as 'either Oxford or Cambridge'.[6] To Americans, Hill simply sounded English. Like her Soviet-born colleague in Trump's National Security Council, Alexander Vindman, she had had to emigrate to advance.

Other British scholars returned home from Harvard with the latest in centre-left policy thinking, which they helped deliver to a grateful Tony Blair and Gordon Brown, then busy remaking the Labour Party. Several New Labour ideas – such as the New Deal for the long-term unemployed, or Sure Start, the programme for toddlers – had American intellectual origins.

*

The Oxford Tories didn't bother with graduate school. As per public-school tradition, they seemed to feel that Oxford had completed their formal education. As straight white men, they were (in the unmatched phrase of the writer John Scalzi) playing the game called *The Real World* with the difficulty setting on 'Easy'.[7] They could march into adulthood and do whatever they liked.

Johnson's first step on his planned post-university path was to get married. Late in 1987, the student magazine *Isis* (previously edited by Rachel Johnson) sketched a picture that would be familiar to almost everybody in Britain thirty-five years later:

> It has been one of the trademarks of Boris Johnson to turn shambling eccentricity into a smart career move. It helped win the Captaincy of Eton, the Presidency of the Union, and the hand of socialite Allegra Mostyn-Owen. Their wedding this summer in Shropshire seemed to mark a new stage in his life. For once Boris was in control.
>
> But, as guests enjoyed the lavish reception, Boris and Allegra set off for their honeymoon to spend their wedding-night NOT in romantic Egypt but in nearby Church Strutton [*sic*; actually Church Stretton]. True to form, Boris had completely forgotten that one needs visas to visit Egypt.[8]

Whereas many German and American politicians build their careers in the regions, Johnson and the other Oxford Tories headed straight for London. Malcolm Turnbull remarks: 'Apart from city-states, I can't think of another country which is so dominated by its capital as the UK is. Its institutions are national.'

The Johnson–Cameron generation arrived in London in their early twenties already equipped with a map of British power. Looming in the distance was the highest peak: the Palace of Westminster. These men had grown up inside institutions, and the Commons ('the brown, smelly, tawny, male paradise' of the diarist MP Chips Channon)[9] was the sort of medieval Gothic public-school club where they felt at home – or in the case of a middle-class wannabe like Gove, were learning to feel at home. But even they couldn't stroll through the front door aged twenty-one.

At the time, politically ambitious public schoolboys seemed to be flying into a national headwind. Luke Harding, the former *Cherwell* editor, later emailed me: 'I saw the Oxford Union types as ludicrous figures, with extreme pantomime views. I was confident they (and their brand of politics) would fail to prosper.' By the late 1980s, no public schoolboy had led either party since Douglas-Home stood down as Tory leader in 1965. Thatcher had purged the mostly posh 'Wets' from her cabinet. Adonis, as a young politics lecturer at Oxford, predicted that 'there would never be another Etonian in number ten'.[10] Indeed, in 1990, the Old Etonian Douglas Hurd was judged too posh to succeed Thatcher. Despite Hurd's protests that his father had been a mere tenant farmer (albeit farming 500 acres), the job went to John Major from Brixton.[11]

The City of the day – then still very British, even after the Big Bang of 1986 – seemed a cosier upper-class destination than Downing Street. And there was money to be made elsewhere, too. *Cherwell* in the late Thatcher years was full of recruitment ads for management consultancies, accounting and law firms.

Yet the Tory public schoolboys still believed in their political destiny. Harding admits to underestimating 'the energy they had, and the ambition, and the way they went straight to the people in power. What I hadn't realised was how networked they were.' Their party was the most successful election-winning machine in the western world, and they were going to run it. Perhaps toffs could no longer become prime minister, but they could certainly keep their places at the top table. Adonis reflected later: 'Etonians never actually left the Tory high command. They were just tactically moved away from front of stage. Even as I was predicting their demise, an astonishing sixty-one Etonians served as ministers in the Thatcher/Major governments.'[12]

First prize for an ambitious Tory graduate in the Thatcher era was a job at the Conservative Research Department. On 15 June 1988, its deputy director, who was about to interview a young man from Oxford, received a phone call from Buckingham Palace. The caller, who did not identify himself, said: 'I understand that you are to see David Cameron. I've tried everything I can to dissuade him from wasting his time on politics, but I have failed. You are about to meet a truly remarkable young man.'[13] Cameron got the job. Given the Tory grip on Britain then, this was like an ambitious twenty-one-year-old Soviet being assigned an office in the Kremlin. Michael Gove, who left Oxford that same month, applied to the Research Department too, but was rejected as 'insufficiently conservative' and 'insufficiently political'.[14]

George Osborne wanted to become a journalist, but was turned down for *The Times*'s graduate scheme.[15] Only after that did a friend alert him to a gig at the Conservative Research Department, where he met Cameron, his caste-mate and fellow Bullingdon alumnus. It was a posh office, recalls David Allen Green, who was interviewed for a job there by Cameron in 1994. Green had attended Birmingham state schools before Oxford, and says, 'I've never felt so conscious of my social and economic background in my life. And I wasn't taken on.'

Osborne was later rejected for a job at *The Economist*[16] (where Cameron had also interviewed).[17] It would take decades and the intervention of the Russian owner of the *Evening Standard* before he could live his journalistic dream.

But most of the Oxford Tories did go into the rhetoric industries. Gove, after an interview with the *Telegraph*'s editor Max Hastings, started out on the newspaper's Peterborough Diary – a traditional post-Oxford post, where the brief was generally to write about upper-class Bright Young Things whom most readers hadn't heard of. Gove's connections were so weak that he had to make a rare regional detour (to his native Scotland), but he soon established himself in London with *The Times*. He began attending meetings of Dan Hannan's ERG.[18] He was still in his twenties when Rupert Murdoch spotted his potential.

Boris Johnson didn't have Cameron's royal route to power, and seems to have considered himself disadvantaged by comparison. He lasted a week in management consultancy.[19] He then joined *The Times*, where he and Toby Young were fired in quick succession, in Johnson's case for making up a quote from his godfather, the historian Colin Lucas. This might have ended another young journalist's career, but during Johnson's tenure as Union president in 1986, he had invited Max Hastings to speak at a debate. Hastings had been impressed by him, remembered, and hired him for the *Telegraph*'s leader-writing desk, which was staffed by public schoolboys and known inside the building as 'Club Class'.[20] As per upper-class tradition, Johnson had got his career break through personal connection rather than open application. In 1989 he took his shaky French to Brussels to write funny articles about the European Economic Community. He invented a genre of often bogus articles about 'Brussels bureaucrats' who bossed Britons around, regulating banana shapes and condom sizes. His mocking of rules expressed his caste's core belief: nobody tells us what to do.

Charles Moore succeeded Hastings at the *Telegraph*, and recruited from much the same pool. He later recalled: 'I first met Boris at the Oxford Union. It's the only time I've met a president of the Union who I thought was really, really interesting. We talked about creationism.'[21]

After Hannan left the ERG, Moore hired him as a leader-writer, too. Owen Matthews recalls: 'The less prodigiously intelligent would go and work on the Diary pages, and the intellectually more able would go straight to the Leader desk, because it's just like Oxford essay-writing.' The Labourites Yvette Cooper, Ed Balls and Adonis also joined national newspapers. Rees-Mogg as a student had dabbled in London journalism,[22] and he considered it as a career, but, he says, 'Frankly, I wasn't as good at it as my father.' William Rees-Mogg had been editor of *The Times*. Jacob went off to Hong Kong to work in finance.

When I asked Hannan why a group of people who could have chosen any career flocked to Grub Street, he replied: 'I'd always wanted to write columns. At the time that I applied for the *Telegraph*, I just thought that was what

I was going to do for the rest of my life.' Rachel Johnson, who started her career at the *Financial Times*, observes that becoming a journalist, especially a columnist, allowed 'a kind of projection of personality that going into a merchant bank or a management consultancy didn't offer. It was the beginning of the cult of personality and of the development of your individual brand.'

In 1994 Cameron followed the others into the rhetorical sector, where he ran public relations at the media company Carlton Communications.[23] These men were honing their media techniques, which were replacing the debating skills of older Oxford Tories such as William Hague as the politician's essential weapon. They learned more about the mechanics of TV soundbites than about, say, global supply chains.

At this point I was still on much the same track as they were. Like them, I had built my career on the British system of Oxbridge males recruiting each other. When I applied to the *Financial Times* in 1994, I think I was interviewed only by straight white Oxbridge men (except for one who came out of the closet a few years later). That was the tradition. When the Ulsterman Walter Ellis applied to the *FT* in 1979, he had been 'bemused not merely to be asked when I had gone up to Oxford but, more importantly, which college I had attended'. In fact, Ellis had dropped out of school and two non-Oxbridge universities. The *FT* hired him regardless. He eventually resigned after realising that staff from redbrick universities were treated as 'office juniors'.[24] The year I joined the *FT*, Ellis published his book *The Oxbridge Conspiracy: How the Ancient Universities Have Kept Their Stranglehold on the Establishment*.

The *FT* of the 1990s, like most British establishment institutions at the time, operated on a Brahminesque caste system: editors and writers had been to Oxbridge, sub-editors to other universities, while support staff typically hadn't attended university at all. I learned that the British ruling caste refreshed its talent base by maintaining a small fast track for exceptionally talented commoners, preferably ones who came in a reassuringly white, male, Oxbridge packaging. My first boss at the *FT* was Andrew Adonis. It took me one lunch with him to establish that he was three times cleverer than me. Tony Blair spotted the same fact, and the Cypriot postman's son soon left the *FT* and ended up a cabinet minister. A few months later I was working on the *FT*'s foreign desk under Robert Thomson, a small-town Australian who had initially skipped university to become a seventeen-year-old copy-boy at the *Melbourne Herald*. Thomson was approximately as clever as Adonis. Rupert Murdoch poached him and made him editor of *The Times*, and later chief executive of News Corp.[25] My last boss in the building, Robert Chote, a middle-class economics whizz from Southampton, went on to spend a decade chairing the Office for Budget Responsibility.

I wasn't made for greater things. Stuck all day in an office where the windows didn't open, I eventually hit on a trick that worked best for white Oxbridge males: go off and live my life while leaving a suit jacket draped permanently over my empty chair, so that whenever a boss walked by, generally a fellow white Oxbridge male, he'd think, 'Ah, Kuper, good chap, working all hours.' My start in journalism was unimpressive, but then I didn't have much to prove: I already was a white Oxbridge male. About the

same time as I began work, a black non-Oxbridge friend
started out as a reporter at another national newspaper.
His news editor had little confidence in him. My friend
never advanced very far. Perhaps I now have his career.

12

OUR HOUSE

I think the Union does help you an enormous amount.
I remember when I first went into the House of
Commons in 1950, I felt I was coming home.

Edward Heath[1]

The Oxford Tories belonged in journalism. Opinion-writing was exactly what their education had prepared them for. The right-wing *Spectator* magazine became their London clubhouse. The American journalist Anne Applebaum, who worked for the *Spectator* from 1992 to 1996, recalled: 'The tone of every conversation, every editorial meeting, was arch, every professional conversation amusing; there was no moment when the joke ended or the irony ceased.'[2] In 1999, Johnson became editor of the magazine.

By this time, he had transferred his Oxford Union persona to the TV screen, starring in the show *Have I Got News For You*. His style turned out to work on a national stage. Ian Buruma writes,

Johnson deliberately exaggerated the upper-class

mannerisms he acquired at Eton and Oxford: the stammering drawl, the self-deprecating jocularity that can only come from a deep reservoir of assumed superiority, the cultivated amateurishness, the Latin quotations, the carefully studied slovenly dress ... Johnson realised that playing down his upper-class education would only make him look shifty, and so he played it up.[3]

Meanwhile, he maintained his Union ties as a celebrity visitor. After a debate in 1998, a bottle of Holsten in hand, he lectured a Dutch television crew on the benefits of the chamber's adversarial layout: 'You all sit around in your sort of little semicircles, in Holland or wherever you come from, all being nice to each other. And, you know, great pathetic coalition governments you produce – immensely corrupt.'[4]

Entertainment journalism was the perfect role for a man who lacked the patience for serious political ideas. His long-time neighbour in Islington, the political thinker David Goodhart, observed of him: 'He mocks everything, particularly ideas and thoughts that he calls -isms.'[5] Any theory that couldn't be set out in an elegant 800-word *Spectator* column deserved to be dismissed as 'boring' – a core word in the upper-class vocabulary – and laughed out of the room. This was a general tendency among Tories. When Gordon Brown, advised by Ed Balls, used the phrase 'neoclassical endogenous growth theory' in a speech in 1993, Heseltine told a delighted Tory conference: 'It wasn't Brown's. It was Balls!'[6]

Life was good at the *Spectator*. And yet Johnson was

preparing the leap into the senior branch of the rhetorical sector: parliament. As he explained, 'They don't put up statues to journalists.'[7]

Luckily, the Conservative Party operated the traditional British inside track for Oxbridge public schoolboys. Rees-Mogg says that before the 1997 election, when he was about twenty-seven, 'I came back from Hong Kong and discovered that quite a lot of my friends were standing in seats that it was improbable that they would win, and I thought, "Gosh, well, if they can do it, I can do it".'

Tory selection panels tend to like posh men with pukkah CVs. Cameron and Johnson in 2001, and Gove in 2005, were handed safe seats in wealthy parts of southern England. MPs with safe seats have the best shot at a ministerial career, because Whips don't want to give a big job to somebody who will have to rush back to their constituency every time there's a controversial planning meeting.

And people who arrived in the Commons as celebrities – above all Johnson, but even Gove, who had been a name at *The Times* – had the fastest track of all. They entered politics with a ready-made national constituency outside their own party, and with journalist friends who could help build their profiles. Ex-journalists also had the precious advantage of never having run anything – no company, local government, or colony like their forefathers. They didn't have a record that could be attacked.

The Tory inside track worked best for men, as Rachel Johnson discovered when she briefly joined the party in 2011:

I was told by David Davis that they wanted me to be an

MP and would I join the A-list and I would be a shoo-in, and I was so repulsed by the whole process that I didn't follow through. The application form alone was enough to put you off. I had very small children, and the form sort of said: 'List the examples of all the times you have helped the Tory Party, campaigned for the Tory Party, leafleted etc.' There wasn't a space for saying anything else, really. I thought: 'They just want people who are Tory drones, the kind of guys you would see on Saturday trailing after the MP, handing out leaflets, in a pack.' And I wasn't going to put in that shoe leather. I couldn't anyway. I had small children. And I thought it was so restrictive and so exclusive and so anti-female that I threw it across the room.

When her male contemporaries walked into the Commons, there was no disorienting first-day-at-school moment. Cameron and Johnson already knew each other and many of their new colleagues from school, Oxford, journalism, and evenings out with mutual friends. The Commons was designed for men of their class. It had ancient bylaws, bars, few ladies' rooms and, at the time, no childcare facilities.[8] The debating rules, confrontational layout and heckles were all familiar from the Oxford Union.

Union alumni who arrive in the Commons 'have already been there', writes Fiona Graham, even if parliament required a slightly greater pretence of seriousness.[9] Their Oxford experience gave Johnson et al. several years' head start over rival new MPs. They could get on with setting themselves up as heads of Tory factions. Johnson had the additional advantage of periodic scandals, which he defused with irony and which built his name recognition. He spun rule-breaking as an upper-class prank, like stealing a policeman's helmet on Boat Race Night. His Bullingdon ethos had survived intact, its truth validated by his life path: *The rules don't apply to our class.*

Nor did constituency life deliver great shocks. Many Oxford politicos have their first encounters with ordinary Britons only after becoming MPs. Suddenly they find themselves trekking into the provinces to visit their 'local' schools and hospitals, or to have surgery meetings with constituents who aren't getting their unemployment benefits or social housing or care for a mentally ill relative. Being an MP can be a lot like being a social worker. For Macmillan, becoming MP for poor industrial Stockton in 1924 was his second awakening after the trenches. (Until he campaigned there, he later wrote, 'I had never been to Tees-side or even Tyneside'.) While giving his Oxford Unionesque speeches in Stockton, he 'was surprised to be heckled continuously in a language he barely understood', wrote his biographer, Charles Williams.[10]

But Cameron in Witney, Johnson in Henley and Gove in Surrey Heath didn't meet too many struggling people. And a posh celebrity in a safe seat can easily hand off constituency surgeries to an aide. If you're an MP in this category, explains Sam Gyimah, the former Tory minister, 'people are fortunate to meet you, they are fortunate for you to have time to listen to their housing benefit problem'.

At this point in their evolution, the Oxford Tories hadn't yet found a great political cause to match Empire or the Second World War or even the Thatcher revolution. After all,

Thatcher had already fulfilled most of their policy desires. There wasn't much room left for more privatisation or tax-cutting if Britain were still to remain a recognisable western country. That left the new generation of Tories with little to put right.

Their strongest ideology was a vague yearning for lost British greatness. Applebaum writes: 'They believed that it was still possible for England to make the rules – whether the rules of trade, of economics, of foreign policy – if only their leaders would take the bull by the horns, take the bit between their teeth, if only they would just do it.'[11] When the Iraq War rolled around, the Oxford Tories reflexively backed the invasion.

But in the Blair years, what they thought scarcely mattered anyway. With Labour seeming to have usurped the role of permanent ruling party, the Oxford Tories had no obvious prospect of power. They were competing against the UK's longest period of economic growth in two hundred years. Britons in the late Blair era had unprecedented riches, education and personal freedom. Around this time, a friend said he realised the UK had never had it so good when his postman bought a second home in South Africa. In July 2005, days after the '7/7' bombings of London, one Oxford Tory public schoolboy admitted to me: 'Can I honestly say after last week that I wouldn't want Blair to be PM? No! Frankly, we're pretty well governed.' That summer, Gove told me: 'I am – probably more than most of my colleagues – an admirer of lots of things about Blair.'

I had interviewed these men for a feature I wrote in the *FT*, after the Tories' third straight election defeat that June.

My editor's brief had been: can this party ever recover, or has it been made redundant by modernity? As the Tories prepared to elect yet another new leader to replace Michael Howard, I went to see one of the candidates, a thirty-eight-year-old Etonian who had only been an MP for four years. The moment the fleshy-faced, expensively dressed David Cameron walked into the poky meeting room at Westminster, I looked up at him and he looked down at me, and we each clocked at a glance, as only Britons can: 'He's upper-class!' 'He's middle-class!'

Cameron opened with an ice-breaker: 'For the *FT*, is it? Is it for *How to Spend It*?'

How To Spend It is the *FT*'s monthly luxury magazine, aimed at investment bankers and their spouses. I was not a regular reader. As I began to explain confusedly that I was actually writing for the main paper, Cameron interrupted. 'I'm only joking,' he chortled. 'My wife works for Smythson's. They're always trying to get into *How to Spend It*. It's like "the place to be" if you're a luxury goods business.' He was cack-handedly applying what his schoolmate James Wood called 'the Etonian's uncanny ability to soften entitlement with charm'.[12]

I looked up Smythson later. It was a company in Bond Street that made luxury stationery. Cameron's wife, Samantha, product of a 300-acre estate, was its 'creative director'. In their circles, *How to Spend It* was presumably ubiquitous. He had established our difference with a single quip.

When I asked him whether poshness might be an electoral liability, he rolled out his prepared answer: 'I had a, you know, a great education, and a very ahhm kind and loving upbringing in a wonderful family. I think what matters is what the message is, and what you're going to do in the future. And I just think that's the sort of country I want to live in, where we judge people by what they're going to do, rather than where they've come from.' In other words, he turned class snobbery on its head: don't 'diss' me just because I'm from Eton.

For almost all the thirty-minute interview, Cameron dished up pre-cooked content-free clichés. The fact that he was obviously intelligent only made it more insulting. He was for 'modern compassionate conservatism', he was against 'turning the clock back', and he cautioned: 'You can't rely on the state to do everything, but you can't rely on individuals to do everything.'

So vacuous was the interview that I assumed that in this campaign he was merely making his name so as to run for leader next time around. But it turned out that the Conservative Party wasn't looking for a leader with policies anyway. It just wanted someone who wouldn't run a resistance movement against the zeitgeist. Previous party leaders had spent their energy trying to shred gays, foreigners, young people and single mothers like so many foxes. The Tories had learned, painfully, that that didn't work.

When MPs chose Cameron as the first privately educated Tory leader in forty years, Johnson was irked. It felt like an overturning of the natural order. Cameron had been below him at school and Oxford, and hadn't won many glittering prizes, whereas Johnson had been captain of Eton and president of the Union. Yet the junior protagonist – aided by White's and Buckingham Palace – had triumphed in their personal class struggle. Meanwhile, Howard had just sacked Johnson as party vice-chairman for lying to him about an affair. Johnson was also aggrieved that Gove, the Jeeves to his Wooster, had somehow leap-frogged him in the party.

In 2008 Johnson got himself elected mayor of London, reworking his winning Oxford Union campaign by running as a loveable non-partisan; he barely mentioned the word 'Conservative'.[13] But even as mayor he continued to yearn for his ancestral mothership, the Commons.[14]

After Cameron became leader of the opposition, I wrote in the *FT*: 'I don't believe he can win the Conservatives an election, because he is too blatantly posh.' He then surrounded himself with what Gove called a 'ridiculous' and 'preposterous' number of Old Etonians, notably Ed Llewellyn, Oliver Letwin and Jo Johnson. 'More boys from Eton go to Oxford and Cambridge than boys eligible for free school meals', noted Gove.[15] It's not simply that Cameron felt comfortable with Etonians. It's also that he felt uncomfortable with most other Britons: just look at his interactions with me and David Allen Green, both of us at least Oxford men of his generation. Much more than for Boris Johnson, Eton was Cameron's tribe.

One continental European prime minister, a man of ordinary origins, invited to Chequers by Cameron, real-ised in an evening that the colleague he had got to know from European summits as an informal, cheery, pragmatic chap like himself was in fact a quasi-aristocrat who ruled the UK with a posh clique of school chums. At one point in the visit, the European leader, discombobulated by the accents and the country-house setting, turned to an adviser and muttered: 'If you and I had been born in the UK, we wouldn't be sitting here.'

It's true that Cameron sometimes cast his net wider in the war for talent: his gatekeeper Kate Fall hadn't been to Eton, while his director of strategy, Steve Hilton, was the son of divorced Hungarian parents and had grown up poor. On the other hand, they were both privately educated Oxford PPEists. There were almost no leaks or squabbles inside Cameron's team. Nor were there many alternative viewpoints.

When the electorate proved me wrong in 2010 and put a toff in Downing Street, I had to recalibrate my thinking. Of course, the power of Eton and Oxford does sometimes irritate voters, just as many Americans recoil at 'Harvards' and French voters have got tired of Enarques. But I finally grasped that there is also a conflicting voice in voters' heads saying, 'These chaps were born to rule.' One of the psychic costs imposed by Oxford on ordinary Britons is that many of them come to assume their own inferiority relative to its graduates. My mother, who had been at school and university in South Africa, used to lie awake in middle age and wonder whether, had she been seventeen and British, she would have got into Oxford. 'And the thing is, I don't think I would have.'

Cameron hadn't simply been thrust by his fellow MPs on a grumpy public. Rather, he emerged from Eton and Oxford branded – in his own mind and those of his voters – as a 'leader'. A profile in the *FT* called him 'a man whose most visceral political belief is that he is the best person to run the country'.[16]

Eton and Oxford were electoral assets to Cameron

more than they were weaknesses. Rachel Johnson says, 'You just looked at him and thought, "That is a prime minister". He inhabited the role so easily.' Much of the public certainly liked that. It's noticeable that the only three post-war British prime ministers without an elite educational institution to their name – Callaghan, Major and Gordon Brown – didn't exude ease in office. Perhaps 'leadership ability' is in part simply the ability to feel like a leader.

Cameron's most dangerous rivals were men of his own class. Sam Gyimah, who served as Cameron's parliamentary private secretary and later as a Tory whip, recalls 'how many of the plots to unseat him as leader came from Etonians'. By contrast, a state-school boy like David Davis was never likely to oust Cameron.

Advertising oneself as born to rule has to be done obliquely. Cameron and Boris Johnson both use Eton and Oxford when networking with fellow insiders, but they almost never mention their alma maters in public, in order not to annoy outsiders. So Johnson greets the Polish politician Radek Sikorski, a fellow Bullingdon Club alum, with 'gorilla-like cries' of 'Buller, Buller, Buller!',[17] but warns an old friend with whom he is reminiscing about Oxford days, 'Omertà, omertà'.[18]

Happily for these men, they have never needed to remind anyone of their origins. Cameron's accent, confidence, height and pink rude health always screamed Eton. Johnson plays the Eton type as postmodern satire, but he plays him nonetheless. Bizarrely, though, the Labour Party – itself fronted in the early 2010s by four people who had attended both Oxford and Harvard – clung to the notion that voters were fed up with elites. Labour was always taunting Cameron as 'out of touch'. When Ed Miliband was leader, he even made the fateful decision to have himself photographed eating a proletarian bacon sandwich. He didn't merely look silly. He looked misguided, too. If voters wanted to be led by proletarians, they would vote for proletarians.

13

NO FIGHTING IN THIS ESTABLISHMENT

*'The British establishment uses the royal
we, as in, "We think this"'.*
John Pilger, Australian journalist, 2007[1]

Cameron's Oxford skills served him well as prime minister. A civil servant who worked in Downing Street at the time told me that like Blair, he could digest within minutes a brief about a subject he'd never encountered before, then walk into an international summit or a bilateral meeting and argue it convincingly. The civil servant added that Gordon Brown could do this too, but had the irritating habit of arguing against the briefs he had been given: 'Aha, but there's a paper by a Princeton economist from 2003 that invalidates your position.' Blair and Cameron were emptier vessels, and therefore easier to steer.

As well-spoken Oxonians, they were the perfect front-men for what through most of modern history has been a unified British ruling caste. It has had different labels over time. The early nineteenth-century radical William

Cobbett called it 'The Thing', or 'OLD CORRUPTION'. The Victorians called it the 'upper ten thousand', a body that united all the country's leading ranks. A. N. Wilson sums them up as 'the aristocracy, the literary and political classes, and those educated at the universities.' Much of the point of 'education' for the Victorians, he adds, was to unite these groups into a single club.[2] In the 1950s this club became known as 'the establishment', and now it's 'the elite'.

Club members have traditionally been discouraged from holding strong fixed beliefs. The basic ideology has always been: trust in the system. After all, the system is run by chaps like them, who were at college a couple of minutes' walk from each other. Unlike countries with multiple power centres like the US or Germany or Italy, the UK has a single ruling class.

'You get a homogeneity in your elite that you don't get in larger nations,' remarks Malcolm Turnbull. He adds that even Australia, with a population less than 40 per cent the size of Britain's, is 'a much more diverse country in terms of people's perspectives and attitudes and where they'd been educated, where they went to school, where they grew up.'

Because Britain has no recent traumas of revolution, civil war or collaboration, establishment members traditionally treat each other as good chaps even when they disagree on matters of life and death. In Anthony Powell's twelve-volume novel sequence *A Dance to the Music of Time*, there's a dinner party that takes place just after Chamberlain's return from Munich. Powell, an Eton-and-Oxford man who knew half the establishment, describes two Conservative MPs on opposite sides of the appease-ment debate behaving towards each other with impeccable politeness. They 'had evidently no wish for argument', writes Powell.[3] That's the British establishment. Even the rupture of Munich soon healed, as did the rupture of Thatcherism once New Labour accepted her legacy of pri-vatisation, lower taxes and higher inequality.

By the Cameron years, Britain was once again run by a group of politicians, civil servants, business people and financiers who agreed on most things. The right and left wings of the establishment got along fine. This was not America.

Almost everyone in the twenty-first-century establish-ment was clever, as by this time, even toffs needed brains to get in. The majority on both right and left had pro-gressed from Oxbridge (most commonly PPE at Oxford) to London, where they met at receptions and at each other's kitchen tables. Links between different sectors were close and informal, even when not forged at Eton. Blair's former adviser Alastair Campbell and the Goldman Sachs economist Jim O'Neill (a postman's son) were both friends of Manchester United's manager, Alex Ferguson, who had Blair's mobile number for emergencies.

The ruling caste could accommodate almost anybody. Even 'God Save the Queen' by the Sex Pistols, the ulti-mate anti-establishment song, was played at the Olympic opening ceremony in 2012, the happiest moment of Cam-eron's tenure. I witnessed the same agreeableness lower down the establishment ladder. In 2009, a business school professor and I co-authored a book about football and eco-nomics. A friend who was a leading figure in various far-left organisations threw us a launch party in London. His far-left pals staffed the bar, and listened civilly as my co-author and I pontificated. If they saw us as agents of capital, they were impeccably polite about it. That evening would not have happened in Italy, where the left and agents of capital do not throw each other launch parties.

In the Britain of Blair and Cameron, almost all establishment members shared the same set of facts and, to a large degree, even opinions, which they absorbed every morning from Radio Four's *Today* programme. Almost all had come to accept Britain's place inside the EU but outside its main projects: the euro, Schengen and ever-closer political union. Almost all agreed that social inequality and climate change were big problems, and also agreed not to do anything much about them.

Nobody worried much about the small group of eccentric rebels on the Rees-Moggian Tory right. To Cameron, says Gyimah, 'they seemed like the mad relatives you shut up in the attic. They were people who spoke at length on Fridays in the Commons, when nobody else was there, about private members' bills that no one else cared much about, entertaining each other.' The eccentrics were clearly going nowhere.

Oxbridge men used their establishment podiums to issue ritual laments about the power of Oxbridge men. But they struggled to feel this viscerally. Cameron may genuinely have believed that other people ought one day to get a crack at ruling Britain. However, he and his school-friends were understandably keen to hang on to their own spots. Oxbridge males weren't going to make the revolution, even if they were willing to enlarge their caste a little, generally by admitting a few Oxbridge women. The British establishment has gradually raised the age at which upper-middle-class females hit the glass ceiling: from zero, to seventeen after they were allowed proper schooling, to twenty-one once they were let into Oxbridge, and eventually to thirty-eight when most are still shunted on to the maternity track.

Members of the unified establishment helped each other throughout life. Once, in a faraway land, I visited the British ambassador. Lo and behold, he was a straight white Oxbridge-educated male. He was like a friend I'd never met. He ended up giving me a briefing in his swimming pool.

Having a unified establishment had a soothing effect on national life. But there were downsides, too. Firstly, a unified establishment easily falls prey to groupthink – 'much more of a problem in the UK than it is in Australia', says Turnbull. Almost the entire British establishment, right and left, came to believe in the invasion of Iraq and in the 'light-touch regulation' of banks.

And the establishment's high levels of internal trust were easy to abuse. Take the Libor scandal of 2012, which centred on a bankers' scheme to manipulate the London Interbank Offered Rate (LIBOR) for profit. Only in a unified establishment, where the Bank of England assumed that commercial bankers were good chaps, would they be allowed to 'estimate' a fantastically important interest rate on good faith. Who would have thought that some of them would take advantage?

When ruptures hit Britain in 2015/16, the leaders of the unified establishment of the Cameron era weren't equipped to handle them. 'Politics, to them, is the incremental refinement of the mixed economy in a world where most people agree on most things,' wrote my *FT* colleague Janan Ganesh. But these people were 'unprepared for the surge in Euroscepticism, nativism, violent fanaticism and great power rivalry'. During the Brexit referendum, wrote Ganesh, they looked 'like lab technicians sent to war'.[4]

14

BREXIT AND THE OXFORD UNION

*Every great social movement, every war, every revolution,
every political programme, however edifying and
Utopian, really has behind it the ambitions of some
sectional group which is out to grab power for itself.*
George Orwell, 'Second Thoughts on James Burnham'[1]

Cameron's calling of the referendum echoed Tony Blair's
decision to fight in Iraq. Both men at a fateful moment
were at the peak of their powers: forty-nine years old,
winners of two straight elections, the prime ministership
apparently theirs for as long as they wanted it. All their
lives they had confounded the whingers. Almost everything they had ever touched had turned to gold. When
the issues that would destroy each of their reputations
came up, neither man had thought very hard about it,
but then they had learned in life that they didn't need to:
their Oxford rhetorical skills always carried them through.
The establishment would surely unite behind them, as it
traditionally did on matters of war and EU membership.
Cameron calculated that if the Leave cause were led by
non-Oxbridge outsiders like Nigel Farage, Remain would

win. Nobody in the prime minister's Eton-and-Oxford team seems to have sounded a note of panic.

From the other end of the world, Malcolm Turnbull issues his judgement as a fellow professional:

> What I find extraordinary is this rather breezy attitude on the part of Cameron, presumably that they could just wing it in the same way as they did with the Scottish independence referendum. You would think if you were going to put something like that to the people in a democracy in a responsible way, at the very least you'd appoint a Royal Commission, chaired by some distinguished economists. You'd do a full economic analysis. You'd have some parliamentary committees that would consider it. You'd have a ton of work done. You'd have several years of very informed debate. And you would say, 'Well, this is what it could look like. This is our assessment,' and people can vote at the least with some information.

When Cameron called the referendum on 20 February 2016, it was the moment Dan Hannan had been preparing for since his first term at Oxford. 'Power,' as Lenin had said, 'was lying in the streets.' Hannan picked it up. He had ingested so many European treaties, and spoke so well, in such reassuringly Oxonian tones, that he could sail through any tutorial-style inquisition about the dangers of leaving the EU. He defused all objections with plausible-sounding erudition. 'To repeat,' he told one interviewer, 'absolutely nobody is talking about threatening our place in the single market.'[2]

Gove, who had been influenced by Hannan for twenty years, came on board. But Johnson, as in his Oxford Union days, initially couldn't decide whether to back or oppose the motion. Hannan says:

> I spent a lot of 2015 trying to recruit him. It's become fashionable to say, 'Oh, he just had his eye on the main chance, he was working out what would suit him better as a career move.' Just from my own primary evidence: I had several long involved conversations with him, and he was agonising. They were private [conversations], there was nothing performative about this. He was worried that the EU would, as he kept saying, 'give us a kicking on the way out'. On the other hand, the thing that for him was really the supreme test, was this question of sovereignty.

Of course, other motives influenced the Oxford Tories, too. British ministers were used to making the Eurostar journey to the ghastly modernist European Quarter of Brussels. There they would sit in endless meetings in rooms where the windows didn't open, listening to the Latvian environment minister bang on about indirect land-use change.

Brussels is not a storied medieval parliament resounding with witty English rhetoric. The Globish of the European Quarter, full of Franglais words like 'accession' and 'cohesion', is mostly spoken as a second language by technocrats. Brussels is all about laborious consensus-building, not adversarial jousting. For Oxford Tories, the city was the opposite of the English gentlemen's club of Westminster.

Every time they got off the train at the Gare du Midi, they experienced the descent of the UK: from 'Very Well, Alone' to qualified majority voting. And they had no chums among their continental colleagues: whereas their predecessors like Ken Clarke and Denis Healey had been regulars at European political get-togethers, even the most Europhile of the present generation didn't make those trips.

Importantly, Brussels' occasional attempts to tell Britain what to do offended the sense of personal entitlement the Oxford Tories had grown up with. *Nobody* told them what to do. Rules were for other people. In their private lives, in their financial dealings, and at Westminster, these men expected maximum freedom.

Brexit was the sort of grand cause that Johnson and Gove had lacked all their political careers. It would give them a chance to live in interesting times, as their ancestors had. It would raise the tediously low stakes of British politics. It would be a glorious romantic act, like the Charge of the Light Brigade, only with less personal risk. The Oxford Tories would reclaim parliamentary sovereignty, the birthright of their caste, from the Brussels intruders. In private, they understood that Brexit might not work out brilliantly, but Britain had no natural predators and would survive even a blunder. Sikorski, watching his old university chums from Warsaw, remarked that for Poles, the EU wasn't just a game.

Even more personally, the leading British Leavers in spring 2016 were not having the careers they felt they deserved. In part, they treated Brexit as a kind of Oxford Union presidency campaign. Johnson sniffed the chance to unseat his illegitimate Etonian junior.

Gove joined Johnson's slate partly as an outflow of the Oxford class struggle. By Oxford Tory standards, the private-schoolboy-turned-minister felt like a lower-caste outsider who had nothing to offer but brains. Gove had always understood that in the Conservative Party, cleverness was not considered an essential leadership attribute. It was sometimes even a handicap: Britain was not France. Still, during his years as education secretary, he had thought that he and Cameron were chums.

But when Cameron demoted him to chief whip in 2014, lopping £30,000 off his salary on top of everything else, Gove was devastated. He felt that Cameron and his Etonian coterie had treated him 'like staff'. Tim Shipman suggests in *All Out War* that 'the best way to understand Gove and Cameron is to read *Brideshead Revisited*'. Gove is the gifted upper-middle-class achiever Charles Ryder, under the spell of the aristocratic Flytes.[3] When Cameron banished him from Brideshead, Gove wanted revenge. (Steve Hilton appears to have felt something similar after quitting as Cameron's director of strategy in 2012; he, too, went on to support Leave.) Cummings had been Gove's special adviser at education, but was labelled a 'career psychopath' by Cameron and resigned in late 2013.[4] In 2015 he signed up as director of Vote Leave.

Terrifyingly for Cameron, the referendum had split the ruling class. The credentials of Oxford-educated leaders like Johnson and Gove lent Brexit credibility. With these men on board, Vote Leave had a shot at victory. Johnson's CV, accent, confidence and classical tags suggested that he was more than just a funny man. In British terms, he was born to rule. If he was assuring people that 'the cost of getting out would be virtually nil',[5] or if Gove said, 'The day after we vote to leave, we hold all the cards',[6] then surely Brexit couldn't be just a hazardous leap into the unknown?

Brexit has been billed as an anti-elitist revolt. More precisely, it was an anti-elitist revolt led by an elite: a coup by one set of Oxford public schoolboys against other, backed by an Australian Oxford public schoolboy media magnate masquerading as an anti-elitist. Indeed, many voters were willing to entrust Vote Leave with the national future precisely because it was led by an elite.

If Remain was to win, Cameron would have to launch personal attacks on Johnson and Gove. But he didn't want to. He continued to believe in a unified establishment. They were all good chaps, and once he had won the referendum, they would make up again. He wasn't going to fight dirty. He later admitted to George Osborne that 'it was like fighting with one arm tied behind our backs'.[7]

The Oxford Brexiteers struck a frequently irritable cross-class alliance with Farage and the tabloids, who recruited support beyond the Tory base. Hannan says,

> The biggest problem we had, by far, was not anything that Downing Street said, or anything the EU did. The biggest problem we had, all the way through, was the antics of Leave.EU [Farage's vehicle].
>
> If you are suggesting there were these kind of mainstream and slightly dilettante Oxbridge people and then these sort of hardline Leavers, it was the opposite. The dilettantes were the self-styled 'Bad Boys of Brexit' who treated the whole thing as a prank.
>
> I think Farage's ambition was to emerge as a leading

politician from the referendum campaign and he was
much more focused on that than on the outcome of
the referendum campaign, which was a matter of sur-
prisingly little interest to him.

The Leavers faced an uphill struggle to get the population
on side. Hannan's twenty-five-year campaign to get British
voters angry about the European Union had gained little
traction. As Gove admitted to me in 2005, ordinary voters
had never shown much interest. Perhaps they didn't care
whether they were ruled by an out-of-touch elite in Brussels or ditto in Westminster.

Farage understood that appeals to free trade and sovereignty wouldn't win it for Leave. 'It's just not what people
are bothered about,' he said. Hannan's people, he complained, 'seemed to approach the referendum as if it was
an Oxford Union debate. I don't think they have met any
real people in their entire lives.'[8] In the end, Cummings
focused the Leave campaign on two issues that many
ordinary Britons did care about: immigration and the
National Health Service.

In style, though, Johnson in particular fought the referendum as if it were a Union debate: with funny, almost
substance-free hot air. In England, humour is used to cut
off conversations when they threaten to achieve emotional depth or to get boring or technical. Hence Johnson's
famous line on leaving the EU while keeping the benefits
of its single market: 'My policy on cake is pro having it and
pro eating it.' His displays of eccentricity – which were in
fact markers of his upper-class entitlement to break social
codes – were misread by many ordinary Britons as signs of

authenticity. The hair made him (and by extension, Brexit) seem like a harmless joke. He was offering a camp English version of grimmer populist movements elsewhere. He also had a gift for projecting the hedonistic optimism that he felt about his own life on to the entire country. The 'very, very bright future' that he saw for post-Brexit Britain applied in spades to himself.[9]

Timothy Garton Ash, professor of European Studies at Oxford, describes the referendum as 'an Oxford Union debate with the addition of modern campaigning techniques'. He says, 'One of the great things about British public life is that it's irradiated by a gentle sense of humour – but "*chaque qualité a ses défauts*" ['every quality has its downsides'].'

Johnson learned something during the referendum. It turned out that even at the highest level of politics, you could say things that were plainly false – most importantly, that leaving the EU would free up £350 million a week for the NHS – and many voters would either believe it, or, like the crowd at the Oxford Union, wouldn't particularly mind the untruth so long as they liked you. It was an insight he would carry into his future.

⋆

There are certain parallels between the 1980s Oxford Brexiteers and an earlier elite clique: the 1930s Cambridge spies. Kim Philby, Guy Burgess, Donald Maclean, Anthony Blunt and John Cairncross also emerged from an intimate, all-male, public-school network. Four of them were at Trinity College, with Maclean next door at Trinity Hall. Confident enough to formulate a revolutionary world-view despite being ill-informed, the Cambridge Five embraced a utopian cause: Soviet communism. It promised a far-off paradise that they never expected to have to live in themselves. Working towards it was good fun. Philby recalled that after he and Maclean became Soviet agents, Burgess – a charming, dishevelled, blond, Etonian sybarite – felt 'that he was being excluded from something esoteric and exciting. So he started to badger us, and nobody could badger more effectively than Burgess.'[10]

Ralph Glasser, a working-class Glaswegian who came to Oxford as an undergraduate in 1938, observed similar attitudes in his Marxist fellow students. He wrote of his contemporary, Philip Toynbee: 'Being a revolutionary, for his upper-class coterie of the far left, was an elitist game in which, as when playing soldiers in the nursery, *they* must naturally be the commanders; and with total assurance they took it for granted that after the revolution the top places would again be theirs.'[11]

The Cambridge Five were given roles of responsibility because they possessed elite CVs and came off as archetypal British gentlemen (partly through displays of eccentricity in hairstyles, drink and dress). They pursued their utopia for decades, ignoring all evidence that contradicted it, and looking down on the rest of the establishment for its unimaginative thinking. When the spies were finally exposed, British trust in the establishment suffered a lasting dent.

Admittedly, the comparison between the Cambridge and Oxford sets isn't entirely fair: though both betrayed Britain's interests in the service of Moscow, the Brexiteers did it by mistake.

15

MAY I COUNT ON YOUR VOTE?

Life after Oxford is still Oxford.
Sally Littlejohn, Oxford Union librarian, 1982[1]

The moment Brexit was achieved, Johnson and Hannan airily informed the public that immigration would continue after all. No wonder: whether Poles and Bangladeshis lived in unfashionable English provincial towns was a matter of supreme indifference to the Oxford Brexiteers.

A couple of days after the referendum, when I mentioned the economic risks of Brexit in an email to a privately educated Oxford friend, he chastised me: 'You seem unduly concerned about short-term financial impacts. This is a victory for democracy.' I saw what he meant. If you make £200,000 a year, the threat of recession is just an irritation. But if you make £20,000 it's a personal crisis, and if you are making £15,000 then you will worry about still being able to feed your children.

Meanwhile, the Oxford Tories turned out to have no plan for executing Brexit. Johnson spent the Saturday after the referendum playing cricket at the estate of his Eton and Oxford friend, Earl Spencer. In the Oxford tradition, he was winging it.

The main thing was that Cameron's resignation had opened up 10 Downing Street. The Oxford Brexiteers instantly switched from debate to another familiar format: the in-house leadership election. 'May I count on your vote?' The Oxford Union had been perfect preparation for the Tory leadership race: once again, a big chunk of the electorate consisted of fellow politicians, so a candidate had to build support among his peers in an environment where backstabbing is rife. Gyimah, a former Union president, says, 'The mechanics of ascertaining rock-solid support, lukewarm support, weak support is something that most people would have learned putting together a slate in the Union.' No wonder that Hague, another former Union president, had unexpectedly come from behind to win the Tory leadership election of 1997.

As yet another former Union president remarked, the 2016 contest could be described entirely in Union slang: 'Boris knifed Dave. Michael knifed Boris. Theresa and Michael stole Boris's slate. Boris self-binned.'

Just over thirty years after Gove had helped Johnson get elected president of the Union, he became his campaign manager for prime minister. Then the lifelong votary executed a classic Oxford Union act of backstabbing: after late-night plotting with one Oxford contemporary, Nick Boles, at the house of another, Simone Finn, Gove pulled his support from Johnson and announced in public that his eternal hierarchical superior was unfit to be prime minister. It was as if Jeeves had taken Wooster's seat at the Drones Club. Cameron texted Johnson: 'You should have stuck with me mate.'[2]

Gove tried to become prime minister himself, but May

won. She chose as her deputy Damian Green, whom she had met as an eighteen-year-old at OUCA more than forty years before.[3] But she tasked the Brexiteers with executing Brexit. She gave them the key jobs in cabinet, with Johnson as foreign secretary. This was like asking the winners of a debating competition to engineer a spaceship. Most of these people were talkers, not doers. In fact, the doing had been an almost accidental by-product of the talking.

The referendum had skated over boring policy stuff, so even Brexiteer cabinet ministers discovered only afterwards that Britain would have to pay a large divorce bill, that the Irish border was an issue, and that Britain couldn't stay in the single market while ending freedom of movement. Who knew that all real-world choices are suboptimal?

Nor had they thought hard about the problem of striking new trade deals with the entire world. There is a left-wing conspiracy theory that says the Tory Brexiteers were motivated primarily by economics: that their plan was to turn Britain into an under-regulated free-trading offshore libertarian paradise. I don't believe that was their driving motivation. Many of the Brexiteers (especially Rees-Mogg) may well have liked to do exactly that, and they generally wanted to remove any Brussels rules that constrained their freedom of action, but for almost all of them, economics was an afterthought. Brexit was above all their generational grand project designed to protect the powers of their personal fiefdom of Westminster. The rest was just detail – boring issues of governance best left to swotty civil servants. The civil service, led at the time by Jeremy Heywood (history and economics at Hertford College, 1980–83), was the junior executive wing of Britain's Oxocracy.

Anthony Kenny, former Master of Johnson's old college, last saw his old student in May 2017, during his stint as foreign minister. 'As he departed,' wrote Kenny later,

> I reflected ruefully on the college's part in his education. We had been privileged to be given the task of bringing up members of the nation's political elite. But what had we done for Boris? Had we taught him truthfulness? No. Had we taught him wisdom? No. What *had* we taught? Was it only how to make witty and brilliant speeches? I comforted myself with the thought that even Socrates was very doubtful whether virtue could be taught.[4]

Johnson's high verbal intelligence had absolved him from ever developing his analytical intelligence. Concentrated thought could always be sidestepped with a joke. He and his fellow Brexiteers were so poorly briefed that in December 2017 they accepted the principle of Brussels' 'backstop' plan to keep the Irish land border open, before spending much of the next few years fighting their own decision. The Brexiteers failed to debate Brussels into submission, because the EU's negotiators were lawyers who followed rules. Cummings said later that when Johnson struck the Withdrawal Agreement with the EU in 2019, 'he never had a scoobydoo what the deal he signed meant'.[5] It scarcely mattered anyway: in the Oxford tradition, witty and brilliant speeches trumped reality.

There had long been an element of play in Oxford Tory politics. When Osborne encountered political trouble, his characteristic response was, 'Oh look, it's all a game.'⁶ The play element was most obvious in Rees-Mogg, because he hardly attempted to disguise it. During one argument about Brexit with Nick Boles on the House floor, he joked, 'My honourable friend makes a characteristically Wykehamist point. Highly intelligent, but fundamentally wrong.' It's doubtful how many voters knew that 'Wykehamist' referred to Boles's old school of Winchester. Rees-Mogg didn't care. He then took on the Remainer Oliver Letwin, a fellow Etonian: 'And I must confess I've sometimes thought my right honourable friend for West Dorset was more a Wykehamist than of my own school.'⁷

Months later, Rees-Mogg, leader of the House, lay down on one of the front benches during yet another crucial Brexit debate, as if taking a nap. Like a cat rolling on to its back, he was saying, 'I belong here. This is my home.'⁸ No wonder that at one point in the Brexit saga, Caroline Lucas, the Green MP, had to chastise him: 'This is not a parlour game or debating society. These are real people with real lives.'⁹

Well, that's what she thought. In fact, the Oxford Brexiteers were confident that their own class would be okay whatever happened. If your life passage has taken you from medieval rural home to medieval boarding school to medieval Oxford college and finally to medieval parliament, you inevitably end up thinking: 'What could possibly go wrong?' If Brexit didn't work out, the Oxford Tories could always just set up new investment vehicles inside the EU, like Rees-Mogg, or apply for European passports, like Stanley Johnson. As James Wood writes of his fellow Etonians: 'What amazing security: to have always been well-off probably suggested that one would always be well-off.'[10]

Of course, it's not only Oxford Tory politicians who think that way. So do most of my caste of Oxbridge journalists, academics and comedians who narrate British events. We know, deep inside, that whatever happens, we will be fine. Our lot aren't going to end up on zero-hours contracts or queuing at a food bank. No wonder the relentless irony of *Cherwell* carries over into Britain's grown-up media.

Brexit had plunged the country into what by British standards passed for a crisis. For a time, governing Britain became almost impossible. With Jeremy Corbyn leading Labour and the Tory party torn in half over Brexit, the political elite was probably more divided than at any point since Munich. A 'People's Vote' campaign to hold a second referendum on Brexit was organised by Roland Rudd, Oxford Union president in 1985, and Hugo Dixon, a close Etonian friend of Johnson's, until it collapsed amid infighting. At the other end of the spectrum, some Tory Leavers began treating Remainers as the new appeasers.[11] The European Research Group, at this point led by Rees-Mogg, kept trying to defenestrate the Conservatives' own prime minister, the former Remainer May. After one failed coup, her industry minister Richard Harrington (also Oxford, obviously) sneered at the plotters: 'They are like student union kids.'[12] In May 2019, May finally resigned, triggering the next Oxford Union election for grown-ups.

Seven candidates, all men, survived the first round. Six of them – Johnson, Hunt, Gove, Raab, Matt Hancock and Rory Stewart – had studied arts subjects, law or PPE at

Oxford. The sole representative of the rest of Britain, Sajid Javid, son of a Pakistani bus-driver-turned-shopkeeper, had attended Filton Technical College and Exeter University. 'People don't want to see a final that's some kind of Oxford Union debate,' he said,[13] to no avail.

In this company, Rory Stewart looked like a throwback to the Macmillan generation: after Eton and Balliol, he had seen war up close, serving as an administrator in occupied Iraq and later working in Afghanistan. He had observed as early as 2007 that in British politics, 'Churchill has been replaced by Bertie Wooster'. Remarking at the time on Britain's 'pockets of shameful poverty', he wrote: 'I have encountered a level of random hostility, aggression and bitterness in Scottish public housing that I have never seen in an Afghan village.'[14]

Shortly before the leadership campaign started, Stewart produced a stirring rant that expresses some of the themes of this book better than I can:

> I feel that there is a deep lack of seriousness in British politics ... I felt as soon as I saw us debate Afghanistan that we were not a serious country. The people debating it were not asking serious questions. There is a lot of pantomime, on every side. Not only the Conservatives, it's Labour too.
>
> When I was the Africa minister, I was at the despatch box and people would pop up. [Stewart puts on a sonorous voice:] 'What is the minister going to do to stop the terrible civil war in Burundi?' Sit down. 'What is the minister going to do to deal with the human rights abuses in western Cameroon?' Sit down. 'What

is the minister going to do to deal with the situation in Togo?' Right? And somebody needs to say to them: 'We do not have an embassy in Burundi. We do not have an embassy in Togo. We're not going to do anything, about any of these issues, and what fantasy world do you live in to think that we're going to do anything?'... So we need to become more serious again.[15]

Instead, Stewart was quickly knocked out of the leadership race. By the fifth round, only the 1980s Oxford politicos Johnson, Gove and Hunt had survived.

Hunt and his campaign manager Philip Dunne (of Eton, Oxford and the Bullingdon) followed the tactics of Neil Sherlock in his Union victory over Johnson in 1984: they targeted Johnson's lack of 'seriousness'. However, their blows barely landed. In the Tory party as at the Union, it seemed natural that the highest office should go to the most charismatic extant Etonian. As at Oxford in 1985, Johnson ran as a centrist, talking up his liberal reign as mayor of London. Rees-Mogg held a series of dinners at his house to introduce him to Tory MPs.

Johnson had the perfect package to appeal to his party's mostly elderly, rural, English members: Eton signalled 'leader', Oxford signalled 'brains', funny signalled 'English', and his Woosterian diction signalled the lost national golden age. He took Downing Street as he had the Union presidency, with a more competent campaign at the second attempt. On 24 July 2019, he became the fifth Eton-and-Oxford Tory prime minister since 1955. To many who had known him at Oxford, the only surprise was that it had taken so long.

16

THE CHUMOCRACY PANDEMIC

The social system never lets one down.

Captain Grimes in Waugh's *Decline and Fall*

Traditionally in government, the jobs of chief executive and head of communications have been separated. In choosing Johnson, the Tories had merged the two roles. Electorally, this was genius. In the general election of December 2019, the Tories would have had the best words even had they run against someone more fearsome than Corbyn. Cummings came up with another winning slogan, 'Get Brexit done', which spoke to both halves of the exhausted country. He helped Johnson win a five-year term and days later, by his own account, was already trying 'to get rid of him' on the grounds that Johnson 'doesn't have a plan, he doesn't know how to be prime minister, and we'd only got him in there because we had to solve a certain problem'.[1] Unfit as Johnson might be to run Britain, he had already proved himself the equal of Blair and Thatcher in winning campaigns: he had notched up a treble in three years, from the referendum through the Tory leadership race to the general election.

Once Corbyn was gone and Brexit 'done', the English elite began to regain its traditional unity, assisted by Johnson's purges of Remainer Tories. Three years after Gove had stabbed him in the back, Johnson reappointed him his chief votary: after all, they had both learned in the Union that politics was only a game.

Frank Luntz, who had become a regular visitor to his Oxford contemporaries, watched the two of them in action behind the scenes. He says, 'Gove delivered the best PMQ prep I've ever seen in any country. He just took the prime minister apart and helped put him back together again.' But then this government of PPEists, literature students, historians and lawyers, led by a classicist writing a biography of Shakespeare on the side, was hit by a problem for which Oxford had not prepared them: a virus. Suddenly they found themselves confronting questions of biology, statistics and exponential growth.

Once Johnson belatedly began paying attention to the virus, his first instinct was to avoid a lockdown. After all, the main thing his caste had learned to demand from life was maximum personal freedom. The World Health Organization declared the coronavirus a global pandemic on 11 March 2020. France, where I live, locked down on 17 March, several days too late. Johnson kept the UK open until 23 March. Neil Ferguson, at the time a member of the government's Scientific Advisory Group for Emergencies, estimated in June that locking down a week earlier could have reduced Britain's death toll – at that point about 50,000 – by 'at least half'.[2] That would make Johnson's delay possibly the deadliest decision in post-war British history. In October 2021, a report by two House of

Commons all-party committees called the government's initial strategy of pursuing herd immunity and the consequent late lockdown 'one of the most important public health failures the United Kingdom has ever experienced'.[3]

In spring 2020, with death all around, the government found itself in a hole. The UK didn't have enough protective medical gear or Covid-19 tests. A vaccine seemed a distant hope. What to do? The usual thing would have been to work through the civil service, but Cummings, who was essentially running Downing Street during this period, despised the 'disaster zone' of Whitehall[4] with its time-wasting procedures. It was time to move fast and break things. Who could save Britain in an emergency? The people in charge turned to their chums.

I'm sure they didn't perceive this as corrupt. They just needed solutions urgently, and as luck would have it, they knew exactly the people who could help. In fact, they had known them since Oxford. Class solidarity kicked in. Much of Britain's pandemic response was routed through people who had been at university with Johnson et al., then gone into business rather than the soul-corrupting civil service, had married Tories or business moguls, and ended up on the London Tory dinner-party circuit. They were the chums you ran into at friends' children's weddings, or in the paddock at Cheltenham, or out and about in Notting Hill. They were also rare members of the educated elite who hadn't rejected the Tory Brexit project. Appointing them would help build a new Johnsonian establishment. The people in government WhatsApped their chums, or the chums – who had all the right phone numbers – WhatsApped them. It felt like an efficient way to get things done.

The understandably panicked procurement process for personal protective equipment (PPE) such as face masks and gloves ended up wasting £8.7 billion, according to the Department for Health and Social Care's accounts. Among other things, PPE worth £673 million was entirely unusable; another £750 million was spent on items not used before their expiry date, and nearly £2.6 billion on 'items not suitable for use in the NHS' but that might be sold or given to charities; while the value of the department's remaining stock plunged by £4.7 billion as the price of PPE fell. The Treasury judged that £1.3 billion of the department's total spending 'did not have proper HM Treasury consent and was irregular', mostly because 'either the department or NHS England had spent funds without approval or in express breach of the conditions that had been set', wrote the government's auditor.[5]

Dido Harding, an Oxford PPEist, chum of Cameron's and a big shot in British horse racing, was put in charge of the NHS's Test and Trace programme. Soon afterwards she was made head of the National Institute for Health Protection. The non-profit Good Law Project noted: 'Dido Harding didn't pip other candidates to the post at the interview. There weren't any other candidates. She was just handed the job.'[6] An NHS Track and Trace official explained that 'Baroness Harding was hired for her leadership, not her knowledge'.[7] 'Leadership' is of course British code for being upper class. She had also run businesses, albeit not always successfully. Two judges later ruled her NIHP appointment illegal, as Hancock hadn't ensured fair access to the post for others.

Her husband happened to be the Tory MP John

Penrose, who held the official post of 'Prime Minister's Anti-Corruption Champion'. In October 2020, voicing the ruling caste's ignorance of the lives of ordinary Britons, Penrose blamed 'chaotic parents' for sending children to school without breakfast.[8] In his defence, at least Penrose himself doesn't come from Britain's gilded inner circle: he went to Cambridge.

Meanwhile, Johnson's instincts told him to keep reopening England too early, notably promising 'as normal a Christmas as possible' in 2020. Even when he belatedly and reluctantly decreed curbs, the privately educated ruling caste seems to have taken the characteristic view that it was exempt. While ordinary Britons were locked up at home, the rule-makers went on an almost Bullingdonesque tear of rule-breaking: Dominic Cummings's family outing to Barnard Castle in April 2020, and then a seemingly inexhaustible sequence of parties in Downing Street during various national lockdowns. One party in May 2020, attended by about forty people, started fifty-five minutes after the culture secretary, Oliver Dowden, had reminded the rest of England to only meet in pairs outdoors. It was always almost inevitable that the parties would eventually become public knowledge, and that Britons – many of whom had missed funerals or even basic human company during months of lockdown – would then get angry. For Johnson to risk the premiership over office booze-ups might seem like an insane act of self-harm. But he had been getting away with transgression all his life – so much so that an endless string of scandals had built his persona and name recognition and eventually carried him to Downing street. Why would he stop?

His caste instinctively scorned constraints. Had he still been a *Telegraph* columnist, he would surely have been warning the prime minister against imprisoning the nation over a flu. In his absence, that role was taken by other 1980s Oxford Tory journalists such as Toby Young, Julia Hartley-Brewer and James Delingpole. Their lack of scientific training did not impact their intellectual confidence. 'When we have herd immunity Boris will face a reckoning on this pointless and damaging lockdown,' was the headline on Young's *Telegraph* column in July 2020.[9] Six months later, after well over 100,000 deaths, Young's Lockdown Sceptics website still had a section headed 'Where's the pandemic?', which said that 'cases are just positive tests'.[10]

Young, Hartley-Brewer and Delingpole had inherited the role that Hannan, Gove and Johnson himself played over Brexit: a vanguard of skilled wordsmiths can equip the Torysphere with an entertaining and persuasive story, wrapped in Oxford-tutorial level plausibility, larded with quips and choice statistics and appeals to ancient English traditions of liberty, Burke and all that. Boring experts might dissect the message with unmemorable phrases, but they didn't get much of a hearing in the Torysphere. The 'sceptics' as much as the scientists were a voice in Johnson's ear. Of course, an equally powerful voice was the 'Advisory Board' of elite donors to the Conservative Party, who had monthly access to Johnson or Rishi Sunak.[11]

Dido Harding was allocated £37 billion over two years, yet couldn't save the day with Covid-19 testing. Meg Hillier, chair of the Commons Public Accounts Committee, said in March 2021: 'Despite the unimaginable resources thrown at this project, NHS Test and Trace cannot point to a measurable difference to the progress of the pandemic.'[12] By then, the UK's death toll from the virus had topped 120,000 – about three times the number of Britons killed in the Blitz.[13] It was also the highest per-capita rate at that point in the pandemic for any country with more than 12 million people, calculates the Oxford geographer Danny Dorling.[14]

To be fair to Test and Trace, it did produce some winners: above all, the outsourcing company Serco, whose share price soared thanks to government contracts.[15] Serco's chief executive was Rupert Soames, Churchill's grandson, the former Oxford Union president and Bullingdon club member[16] who forty years earlier had announced his ambition to be 'as rich as one can possibly be'. Serco paid him £4.9 million in 2020.[17]

Even after Harding's failure, Matt Hancock, the health secretary, a jockey and horse-racing nut himself, backed her to succeed Simon Stevens as chief executive of NHS England. (Stevens had got the job in 2013 in an earlier iteration of the Oxocracy, appointed by his university PPE contemporaries Cameron and Jeremy Hunt.)

Gina Coladangelo had been in student radio at Oxford with Hancock, so he made her his aide and gave her a £15,000-a-year role as non-executive director in his department. When he was caught in a clinch with her on CCTV camera, breaking social-distancing rules, he had to resign, incidentally dooming Harding's bid to run the NHS.

The chum instinct operated to the last. Amid the disgrace of 'partygate' in February 2022, Johnson tried to rebuild his image by appointing a new communications director: Guto Harri, a contemporary from the Oxford

Union, who retained fond memories of Johnson's 'utterly hilarious' readings of minutes nearly forty years earlier. Starting work at Downing Street, Harri praised Johnson as 'not a complete clown'.[18]

One chum appointment did work out brilliantly. The venture capitalist Kate Bingham was an Oxford contemporary of Johnson, Gove, et al. who married the Tory MP Jesse Norman (Eton and Oxford). Johnson put her in charge of the government's Vaccine Taskforce, and she succeeded. The rapid roll-out of vaccines put a brake on Britain's epidemic before any other western country did so. Still, we have to ask: why did so many Britons die in 2020?

This wasn't a one-off disaster. It was the British state's fourth major policy blunder in less than twenty years, after the Iraq war, the financial crisis and Brexit. Like the previous disasters, and like Johnson's premiership itself, it had its roots partly in the privileging of rhetoric over facts or expertise.

In 2002/3, it had been Tony Blair's articulacy that sold the Iraq war in Britain. When he hinted that Saddam Hussein's imaginary 'weapons of mass destruction' could hit the UK,[19] the ruling class mostly believed him. Educated Americans would often praise Blair for arguing the case more eloquently than President Bush could. Yes: Blair spoke well. That was what he did. Where there were gaps in his knowledge, he talked around them.

Then the financial crisis hit Britain harder than most other countries, largely because London's financial sector was so big. For decades, the mostly innumerate political caste had treated the City as a magic money tree, whose demands always had to be granted because lord knew how the thing actually worked. In 2008, the tree fell over and hit the country. Then came Brexit and Covid-19. Germany, to cite one possible benchmark, either avoided or mitigated all four disasters.

Malcolm Turnbull, surveying Britain in late 2020 from the safety of Australia, remarked: 'The handling of Covid in the UK, I guess, is an example of not handling administration competently or effectively. The once-over lightly, debating chamber style – well, you can skate along for quite a long time, but then you end up with very serious consequences.' It would be nice to think the disasters will prompt change, a sweeping out of the old order, but we all know how Britain works.

17

WHAT IS TO BE DONE?

*We should stop selecting leaders from a subset
of Oxbridge egomaniacs with a humanities
degree and a spell as a spin doctor.*

Dominic Cummings, 2014[1]

'All the glittering prizes were handed out on the basis of what school and what university you went to, in a ceremony that 99 per cent of the population didn't know was even taking place,' says Rachel Johnson. 'That's the truth of the matter. I don't know if it still is. I hope it's not.'

Is this still the truth of the matter? And if it is, how might we change that?

It's an odd feeling to return to a town that you have barely seen in decades, but where you know every street. Whenever I visit Oxford, once every few years or so, I feel like a time traveller. Walking around, I have in my head the university I first encountered as an eighteen-year-old in 1988. I experience a series of small shocks: 'Students are sitting in coffee shops working on laptops! The food is decent! There are Chinese tourists! I'm walking through

Christ Church Meadow checking my emails!' In my day, we didn't even have telephones in our rooms.

The city itself looks almost unchanged, as it will three hundred years from now, and yet the university has moved on. The dilettantish Oxford I knew has been replaced with something quite professional and money-driven. The last time I wandered around my old college, I marvelled at the Chinese, Russian and German surnames at the bottom of the staircases: Oxford is being intellectually globalised. There are about four times more applicants per place now than there were in the 1980s,[2] the students work harder to get in, they want a return on their fees, and they tend to regard Oxford as stage one of their working lives. Many visit the careers service in their first term, rather than just toddling along hungover a few days after final exams. One tutor, who had been a fellow student of mine, said he now tells undergraduates: 'This is your job. You are a full-time undergraduate. You should be doing forty hours a week minimum.' He added: 'And inside I'm thinking back to the weeks when I did two hours. When people of our generation come back, they are really struck by the earnestness. Someone like Boris now just would not get into Oxford.'

Oxford today recruits star academics rather than alcoholics without PhDs. Helpfully, the university has got much richer. In the month I arrived, October 1988, Oxford launched the fundraising 'Campaign for Oxford'. Its aim of raising £220 million in the first five years made it the biggest such campaign ever attempted by an educational institution outside North America.[3] Many dons thought the whole thing impossibly vulgar. But from 2004 through to 2019, the Oxford Thinking Campaign raised £3.3 billion.[4]

Individual colleges all now have their own fundraising operations.

Today the city centre smells of money. Practically the first building you see after getting off the train is the Saïd Business School, named after a Syrian-Saudi-Canadian arms dealer. (His wife, Rosemary Saïd, gave at least £250,000 to the Conservative Party in 2020 or 2021.)[5] Ten minutes' walk away is the Blavatnik School of Government, named after a billionaire businessman from Odessa. Neither school was there in my day. Nor was the Oxford Internet Institute, while the city's two Science Parks only got going in the 1990s.

Most tutors today don't tolerate articulate bluffers. There is even some soul-searching over Oxford's role in shaping the Brexiteers. Louise Richardson, the university's vice-chancellor, has said that she was 'embarrassed to confess we educated' Michael Gove.[6]

Final exams have been reformed to favour scholars over 'natural essayists', a history tutor told me. Partly driven by the gender gap in results – confident men being rewarded for bold counterintuitive arguments made in a hurry – the format of three essays in a three-hour exam, with multiple such tests in a week or so at the end of the third year, is in decline. Now the history degree gives more weight to a compulsory 12,000-word thesis, a 'Special Subject Extended Essay', and a take-home paper at the end of the second year in which students have a week to write three essays.

Covid-19 prompted another reform: after exams were scrapped, history students had to submit revised, improved and footnoted versions of their three best term-time essays. In the 1980s, footnotes on undergraduate essays were almost unheard of. The veteran tutor told me in late 2021: 'We have already abandoned the Covid "portfolio", but we won't go back to a big majority of timed exams.'

All this is progress. 'Thankfully, I do believe that the ethos of the place has significantly changed since the 1990s,' says Kalypso Nicolaïdis, the Oxford professor of international relations. The bigger issue, though, is who gets into Oxford to write footnotes in the first place. Even in the 1980s, there was an unceasing yet leisurely discussion about how to reduce the private-school intake. Somehow, nothing ever seemed to change. It was almost as if the debate itself was the point: everyone got a chance to express their sorrow, as if in a religious absolution ritual, but the same caste stayed on top. Along similar lines, you may vaguely recall Theresa May's expression of concern for the nation on the steps of 10 Downing Street after she became prime minister in 2016:

> If you're born poor, you will die on average nine years earlier than others. If you're black, you're treated more harshly by the criminal justice system than if you're white. If you're a white, working-class boy, you're less likely than anybody else in Britain to go to university. If you're at a state school, you're less likely to reach the top professions than if you're educated privately.[7]

She promised to fight the 'burning injustice'. But then she never found the time. In 2017 Oxford accepted more applicants from Westminster School (49) than black students (48).[8] A study by the Sutton Trust in 2018 found that just eight schools, six of them private, got more places at

Oxbridge than 2,900 other British secondary schools put together. By then, May's cabinet contained more male former presidents of the Oxford Union (Johnson, Gove and Damian Hinds) than people of BME origin (Sajid Javid).[9] The country's elite passes down advantage from generation to generation: 64 per cent of Johnson's first cabinet, in 2019, had attended private school.

Statistics of this kind have become so familiar, like scientists' warnings about climate change, that we barely absorb them any more. Yes, British inequality is dreadful, and it helped prompt the vote for Brexit, but that's the way the system works.

Yet in just the last few years, something surprising has happened: there has been some change. A collection of triggers has belatedly embarrassed Oxbridge into doing something about privilege: first the populist uprising of Brexit, then #MeToo, Black Lives Matter, and the improvement in British state schools. Now, Oxbridge colleges aim for 'contextual admissions', taking account of how much disadvantage candidates have surmounted to reach their academic level. At the start of this century, private schools (which educate about 7 per cent of the population) still supplied about half of Oxford's domestic intake;[10] by 2016, their share had dropped to 42 per cent; by 2020 it was 38 per cent, and only a year later, 32 per cent, the lowest on record.[11] The number of Etonians getting Oxbridge offers fell from 99 in 2014 to 48 in 2021.[12] In 2020/21 Johnson's old college, Balliol, had only one Etonian among its 137 freshers.[13]

Of course, the chief beneficiaries of Oxford's new entry system are upper-middle-class people who choose the state-school route, not the working classes. Fiona Hill reflected: 'Even if I had applied [to Oxford] decades later, I would have been no more likely to have been admitted, since I came from Bishop Barrington Comprehensive School.'[14] Still, the benign scenario – and it is a possibility – is that the Cameron/Johnson era will prove the last hurrah of the traditional ruling class.

Even some sons of privilege themselves now feel an embarrassment that barely existed in the 1980s. One twenty-something told me he didn't put his presidency of the Oxford Union on his CV, because it elicited bad reactions. In 2017 the journalist Harry Mount, a former member of the Bullingdon, reported that the club was 'down to its last two members'.[15] 'No one wants to join', explained the *Telegraph*.[16] In the age of Google and #MeToo, drunken student entitlement can capsize a career. In 2018, OUCA banned Bullingdon members from joining.[17]

Yet even in the 2020s, so much at Oxford remains the same. The outsize role of rhetoric survives. Timothy Garton Ash, professor of European Studies at Oxford, exempts the tutorial system from blame, but says, 'Public schools and the culture around them provide a training in superficial articulacy: essay-writing, public speaking, carrying it off. The Oxford Union reinforces that, even among those who didn't go to public school. Compare and contrast the German elite.'

Nor is Britain's traditional ruling caste about to disband. Among developed countries, possibly only the twenty-first-century US has an elite raised in such isolation from everyone else. British toffs must be hoping that Oxford's new-found egalitarianism is just a fad. As ever, they intend to adapt and hang on. Eton in 2015 built a vast debating chamber,[18] deliberately unequipped with microphones or audio-visual aids so that the boys would learn how to project their voices in preparation for the Commons (which does have microphones). The feeding chain to the Union and on into the Conservative Party survives. Ominously, Jacob Rees-Mogg's Etonian nephew William was president of OUCA in 2017. 'Let's be clear,' the history student in double-breasted suit told the *Telegraph*. 'I am not at all cool.'[19] In 2021 there were still over one hundred Etonians at Oxford.[20]

★

Despite the recent advances, I don't trust Oxford to reform itself. It has served for centuries to funnel privately educated boys from school to the ruling elite. It's an unquestioned component of British power.

Yet it doesn't have to be this way. I have seen myself that a country doesn't need to structure itself around one or two elite universities. I went to a Dutch-speaking school in the Netherlands until the age of sixteen. While I was at Oxford, my childhood friends were at Dutch universities. I used to visit them, and would come home shocked. They had barely any contact with their professors. Where I received one-to-one attention, they would sit in large lecture halls listening to some distant figure drone on. Work, in any case, took up even less of their time than it did of mine. Some of them belonged to fraternities that did little more than drink. I saw Dutch contemporaries drop most of the way out of university to fund their beers through part-time jobs. In those days, the state would sub-sidise them for six years for a degree that was meant to take four.

At Oxford, because I was studying history and German, I spent my third year at the Technical University of West Berlin. I arrived at the end of September 1990, walked among the crowds on Unter den Linden who were cel-ebrating German reunification a few days later, and had a fascinating year, watching the two halves of Berlin grow together. I remember the excitement of Bus 100 being the first to cross the city again since the Second World War. I studied with East Germans who hadn't been able to go to university in the GDR, in some cases because they or their families had offended the regime.

But I learned more from them than I did from my classes at the Technical University. It was much like a Dutch university: unselective, with large classes, and with many students who worked jobs on the side. I sat in class with thirty-year-olds who had been doing their degrees for a decade; one man took his baby into class. I knew a thirty-six-year-old law student who needed to pass just one more exam to graduate. He was doing everything he could to delay taking it, because once he passed he would become a hard-working judge, instead of chilling on his student grant and a few hours a week driving a cab.

Oxford was better than those universities. Partly because it was selective, it had a higher proportion of bright students. And yet the Netherlands and Germany were richer, fairer and more equal societies than Britain. In part, they were fair and equal precisely because their universities weren't selective. Dutch and German children didn't have to be primed by some private school to jump through a hoop aged seventeen. In these countries, there were no university entrance interviews. You studied where you liked, and embarked on hoop-jumping only in adulthood. The judges of Germany's Constitutional Court, for instance, attended a wide range of different universities in Germany and the US. Many came through regional German courts.[21] A map of the origins of Britain's Supreme Court justices would look a lot simpler.

Today, Dutch and German universities are much better than they used to be, but the principle of non-selectivity still mostly applies. In countries without elite universities, where you go simply doesn't matter much. You get a decent education somewhere, and then have to prove yourself in jobs. Careers tend to be decided in adulthood, by which time people's trajectories depend slightly more on their achievements than on their parents.

These countries avoid many British injustices: no doors closed for life at the age of seventeen to almost everyone who doesn't get the letter from Oxbridge. No bitterness as the excluded are slow-tracked through their careers, overseen by an Oxbridge Brahmin caste. No elite households pouring time, money and social capital into getting even undeserving children into Oxbridge. No hysterical private-school headmasters comparing criticisms of their pupils' privileges to Hitler's persecution of the Jews.[22] No disproportionate slice of university funding taken by two institutions. No elite getting clubby, lazy and detached from everybody else because its members sealed themselves off at the age of eighteen.

So far, the British debate about fairness has focused

more on private schools than on Oxbridge. But private schools aren't the whole British problem. You could keep them, and still make the country much fairer. After all, Canada, Australia and Sweden have private schools, but they also have above-average social mobility.[23] Canada, in fact, is the most socially mobile developed country, says the OECD: between 2002 and 2014, nearly three-quarters of Canadians aged twenty-five to sixty-four were in a different social class to their parents.[24]

That's partly because private schooling in these countries doesn't lead to entry into a world-beating university, since Canada, Australia and Sweden don't have world-beating universities, except in a couple of specialist domains. (The Stockholm School of Economics, for instance, is a funnel to the best corporate jobs.) These countries mostly just have lots of good universities, none of which confers a life-changing advantage. The writer Malcolm Gladwell describes applying to the University of Toronto in about ten minutes, 'one evening, after dinner, in the fall of my senior year in high school ... there wasn't a sense that anything great was at stake in the choice of which college we attended'.[25] Imagine that.

*

On 1 January 2022, the elite French postgraduate training school, the Ecole Nationale d'Administration, was formally abolished. ENA, which educated four of the last six French presidents including Emmanuel Macron, as well as both his prime ministers, didn't exactly die. It was converted into an 'institute for public service' that aimed to be 'more meritocratic, more efficient, more in service of democracy'.[26] The hope is that it will no longer just be a place where the French elite reproduces itself for its own benefit.

Britain could do something like that with Oxbridge. There's a lot that's magnificent about these universities. The ideal would be to preserve their excellence, but stop them teaching undergraduates. That would remove Oxbridge's biggest distortion of British life.

Oxford and Cambridge themselves might benefit from the change. They lose money on each undergraduate: the £9,250 in tuition fees doesn't nearly cover costs. If they ditched undergraduates, they could focus entirely on doing research, teaching grad students, spawning tech companies and making even more money from corporate conferences and executive education. Oxford is already moving in this direction: in 2018, for the first time ever, the university had more graduate students than undergraduates. Oxford now claims to have the biggest research budget of any European university, and its research income is about double its income from undergraduate and postgraduate fees. New postgraduate colleges for the sciences and engineering are in the works.

Above all, though, Oxford and Cambridge could educate more excluded Britons. What about retraining gifted but under-qualified adults who never got a chance the first time around, or expanding their summer schools for promising disadvantaged teenagers? Oxbridge for all could raise lots of people's sights. Rather than getting rid of Oxbridge's excellence, we could spread it much more widely.

You might argue that a new set of elite universities – perhaps Imperial College and University College London – would simply replace Oxbridge. Well, it hasn't happened in Canada, Sweden or Australia. Other British universities will always lack Oxbridge's inherited prestige and wealth. It's possible that without Oxbridge, more public school-boys might choose to do their undergraduate degrees at fancy US colleges, but the long-term outcome might be the export of a chunk of the hereditary ruling caste.

Etonians could try to capture Oxbridge's graduate schools, but at least admission there would be from the age of twenty-one – i.e. not simply reflecting parental social class – and education would be more specialist than at undergrad. Doing a PhD in molecular biology or pre-colonial Indian history might not carry you to Downing Street.

Alternatively, we could preserve Oxford unchanged, and just accept elite self-perpetuation as the intended outcome of British life.

NOTES

Introduction: Oxocracy

1. *Cherwell*, 'Union hacks in five in a bed romp shocker', 22 January 1988.
2. *Cherwell*, 'Union slave auction', 12 June 1987.
3. Michael Sandel, *The Tyranny of Merit: What's Become of the Common Good?* (Allen Lane, London, 2020), p. 100.

1. An Elite of Sorts

1. Anthony Sampson, *The Changing Anatomy of Britain* (Coronet Books, London, 1982), p. 165.
2. Susan Hitch, 'Women', in Rachel Johnson (ed.), *The Oxford Myth* (Weidenfeld & Nicholson, London, 1988), p. 88.
3. David Greenaway and Michelle Haynes, 'Funding higher education in the UK: The role of fees and loans', *Economic Journal*, 13 February 2003.
4. Sampson, *The Changing Anatomy of Britain*, p. 164.
5. Michael Gove, 'The President's Address', *Debate*, Hilary term, 1988.
6. Walter Ellis, *The Oxbridge Conspiracy* (Penguin, London, 1995), pp. 150 and 153.
7. Mike Baker, 'Grammar schools – why all the fuss?', BBC News, 2 June 2007.
8. Ellis, *The Oxbridge Conspiracy*, p. 18.
9. Francis Green and David Kynaston, *Engines of Privilege:*

197

Britain's Private School Problem (Bloomsbury, London, 2019), p. 87.

10. Robert Verkaik, *Posh Boys: How the English Public Schools Run Britain* (Oneworld, London, 2018), p. 302.

11. Robert Booth, 'Toby Young: social-media self-obsessive still battling with father's shadow', *Guardian*, 5 January 2018.

12. Fiona Hill, *There Is Nothing For You Here: Finding Opportunity in the Twenty-First Century* (Mariner Books, Boston and New York, 2021), pp. 65–6.

13. Simon Kuper, 'Fiona Hill, Boris Johnson and the tyranny of the plummy British accent', *Financial Times*, 28 November 2019.

14. David Dutton, *Douglas-Home* (Haus Publishing, London, 2006), p. 4.

15. Verkaik, *Posh Boys*, p. 134.

16. Andrew Adonis, 'Importance of being Eton', *Prospect*, 26 May 2021.

17. Quoted in Sebastian Shakespeare, 'Eccentrics', in Johnson, *The Oxford Myth*, p. 52.

18. Ellis, *The Oxbridge Conspiracy*, p. 75.

19. Morris, *Oxford*, pp. 102–3.

20. Andrew Gimson, *Boris: The Rise of Boris Johnson* (Simon & Schuster, London, 2006), p. 55.

21. Allegra Mostyn-Owen, 'Drugs' in Rachel Johnson (ed.), *The Oxford Myth* (Weidenfeld & Nicholson, London, 1988), p. 126.

22. Rosa Ehrenreich, *A Garden of Paper Flowers: An American at Oxford* (Picador, London, 1994), p. 8.

23. Ehrenreich, *A Garden of Paper Flowers*, p. 140.

24. Sampson, *The Changing Anatomy of Britain*, pp. 165–7.

25. Francis Elliott and Tom Baldwin, 'Cameron, Balls and the Oxford crew that is now shaping politics', *The Times*, 23 January 2010.

26. Stefan Collini, 'Inside the mind of Dominic Cummings', *Guardian*, 6 February 2020.

27. John Evelyn, 'Election Special', *Cherwell*, 6 June 1986.

28. Stephen Blease, 'Another little drink ...', *Cherwell*,
    22 November 1991.
29. Ellis, *The Oxford Conspiracy*, p. 62.
30. Susan Hitch, 'Women', in Johnson, *The Oxford Myth*, p. 97.
31. Hitch, 'Women', in Johnson, *The Oxford Myth*, p. 89.

2. Class War
1. E. M. Forster, *Delphi Complete Works of E. M. Forster*
    (Illustrated) Delphi Classics, online.
2. Jan Morris, *Oxford* (Oxford University Press, Oxford, 1987),
    p. 30.
3. Unsigned, 'BMW: A lookback at tension on the frontline',
    Oxford Mail, 17 February 2009.
4. Toby Young, 'Class', in Johnson, *The Oxford Myth*, p. 3.
5. Toby Young, 'When Boris Met Dave: The Bullingdon years',
    Observer, 27 September 2009.
6. Tim Shipman, 'Interview: will Dominic Raab become
    Britain's next prime minister?', *Sunday Times*, 5 May 2019.
7. Retrieved at https://twitter.com/Dominic2306/
    status/1418592811704803331
8. Andrew Adonis, 'State schools and the quiet revolution at
    Oxbridge', *Prospect*, 28 July 2021.
9. Ellis, *The Oxbridge Conspiracy*, p. 287.
10. A. N. Wilson, *The Victorians* (Arrow Books, London, 2003),
    p. 279.
11. Ellis, *The Oxbridge Conspiracy*, p. 52.
12. Richard Beard, *Sad Little Men* (Harvill Secker, London, 2021),
    p. 2.
13. Sonia Purnell, *Just Boris: The Irresistible Rise of a Political
    Celebrity* (Aurum, London, 2011), p. 23.
14. Boris Johnson, 'Politics', in Johnson, *The Oxford Myth*,
    pp. 70–71.
15. Verkaik, *Posh Boys*, p. 293.
16. Danny Dorling, 'New Labour and Inequality: Thatcherism
    Continued?', *Local Economy*, August 2010.

17. Dafydd Jones, *Oxford: The Last Hurrah* (ACC Art Books, Woodbridge, 2020), Introduction.
18. Ian Jack, 'Bright young things revisited: how Cameron's generation made Oxford their playground', *Guardian*, 25 September 2015.
19. John Dower (director), *When Boris Met Dave*, docudrama, 2009.
20. Oliver Taplin, 'Dark Yuppy Blues', *The Times*, 16 June 1988.
21. Purnell, *Just Boris*, p. 62.
22. Andrew Adonis, 'Boris Johnson: The Prime Etonian', *Prospect*, 9 July 2021.
23. Verkaik, *Posh Boys*, p. 135.
24. Morris, *Oxford*, p. 273.
25. Retrieved at https://archive.org/stream/in.ernet. dli.2015.186344/2015.186344.The-Best-Betjeman_djvu.txt
26. Rumeana Jahangir, 'The Hobbit: How England inspired Tolkien's Middle Earth', BBC News, 7 December 2014.
27. Neil Powell, *Amis & Son: Two Literary Generations* (Pan Macmillan, London, 2012), p. 198.
28. Philip Larkin, 'Going, Going' (1972), retrieved at https://www.poeticous.com/philip-larkin/going-going
29. Quoted in Applebaum, *The Twilight of Democracy*, p. 82.
30. Boris Johnson, 'RIP Roger Scruton', Twitter.com, 13 January, 2020, retrieved at https://twitter.com/borisjohnson/status/1 21667426972121907?lang=en
31. Morris, *Oxford*, p. 34.
32. Peter Snow, *Oxford Observed: Town and Gown* (John Murray, London, 1992), pp. 25–6.
33. Retrieved at http://interlitq.org/blog/2014/08/05/t-s-eliot-wrote-to-conrad-aiken-oxford-is-very-pretty-but-i-dont-like-to-be-dead/
34. Sampson, *The Changing Anatomy of Britain*, p. 167.

3. A Little Learning
1. Ian Jack, 'To the miner born', *Guardian*, 27 November 2004.

Notes

2. George Orwell, 'Such, such were the joys', published 1952, retrieved online at https://www.orwell.ru/library/essays/joys/english/e_joys

3. Verkaik, *Posh Boys*, pp. 30–31.

4. Wilson, *The Victorians*, p. 280.

5. Andrew Hodges, *Alan Turing: The Enigma* (Princeton University Press, Princeton, 2015), p. 34.

6. Kitty Ferguson, *Stephen Hawking: His Life and Work* (Transworld, London, 2011), p. 35.

7. Jack, 'Bright young things revisited', *Guardian*.

8. Mostyn-Owen, 'Drugs', in Johnson, *The Oxford Myth*, p. 127.

9. Evelyn Waugh, *Brideshead Revisited* (Penguin Classics, London, 2000), p. 18.

10. Roch Dunin-Wasowicz, 'Are PPE graduates ruining Britain? MPs who studied it at university are among the most pro-Remain', blogs.lse.ac.uk, 14 November 2018.

11. Ellis, *The Oxford Conspiracy*, p. 3.

12. See https://www.ox.ac.uk/sites/files/oxford/Admissions%20Report%202019.pdf

13. Dunin-Wasowicz, 'Are PPE graduates ruining Britain?', blogs.lse.ac.uk

14. Verkaik, *Posh Boys*, p. 283.

15. Walter, *The Oxford Union*, p. 133.

16. Dunin-Wasowicz, 'Are PPE graduates ruining Britain?'

17. Dower, *When Boris Met Dave*.

18. Sampson, *The Changing Anatomy of Britain*, p. 164.

19. David Goodhart, *Head Hand Heart: The Struggle for Dignity and Status in the 21st Century* (Allen Lane, London, 2020), p. 45.

20. Mark S. Bretscher and Graeme Mitchison, 'Obituary: Francis Harry Compton Crick OM. 8 June 1916 – 28 July 2004', Biographical Memoirs of Fellows of the Royal Society, 17 May 2017.

21. Louis MacNeice, 'Autumn Journal', published 1939, retrieved at https://ia801603.us.archive.org/21/items/in.ernet.dli.2015.184237/2015.184237.Autumn-Journal_text.pdf

22. Anthony Kenny, *Brief Encounters: Notes from a Philosopher's Diary* (SPCK Publishing, London, 2018), retrieved through Google Books.
23. Tim Newark, 'Rees-Mogg, an English Trump but better at Latin', *Sunday Times*, 13 August 2017.
24. Quoted in Verkaik, *Posh Boys*, p. 31.
25. Gimson, *Boris*, p. 61.
26. Evelyn Waugh, *Brideshead Revisited*, p. 46.
27. Anthony Kenny, *Brief Encounters*.
28. Richard J. Evans, 'Norman Stone obituary', *Guardian*, 25 June 2019.
29. BBC Radio 4 extra, 'In the Psychiatrist's Chair: Professor Norman Stone, August 1997 (retrieved at https://www.bbc.co.uk/programmes/b0075inr on 17 April 2021).
30. Evans, 'Norman Stone obituary', *Guardian*.
31. Daniel Hannan, 'Where would we now find another Norman Stone?', Conservative Home blog, 30 October 2019.
32. Waugh, *Brideshead Revisited*, p. 6.
33. Jan Morris (ed.), *The Oxford Book of Oxford* (Oxford University Press, Oxford, 1979), p. 380.
34. Morris, *Oxford*, p. 6.
35. Morris, *Oxford*, p. 234.
36. James Wood, 'Diary: These Etonians', *London Review of Books*, 4 July 2019.
37. Morris, *Oxford*, p. 158.
38. Larissa Ham, 'From ping pong to wiff waff, Boris Johnson lauds Team GB', *Sydney Morning Herald*, 25 August 2008.
39. Ehrenreich, *A Garden of Paper Flowers*, pp. 266–7.
40. Ian Buruma, *The Churchill Complex: The Rise and Fall of the Special Relationship* (Atlantic Books, London, 2020).

4. Buller Rules
1. Dower, *When Boris Met Dave*.
2. Unsigned, 'Cameron student photo is banned', BBC *Newsnight*, 2 March 2007.

3. Nick Mutch, Jack Myers, Adam Lusher and Jonathan Owen, 'General Election 2015: Photographic history of Bullingdon Club tracked down – including new picture of David Cameron in his finery', *Independent*, 6 May 2015.
4. Sonia Purnell, 'Jo Johnson is his own man who is very different to Boris', ITV.com, 25 April 2013.
5. Ian Parker, 'Paths of Glory', *New Yorker*, 15 November 2010.
6. Gimson, *Boris*, p. 65.
7. Harriet Sherwood, 'Sexism, vandalism and bullying: inside the Boris Johnson-era Bullingdon Club', *Observer*, 7 July 2019.
8. Ned Temko and David Smith, 'Cameron admits: I used dope at Eton', *Observer*, 11 February 2007.
9. Matt Long and Roger Hopkins Burke, *Vandalism and Anti-Social Behaviour* (Palgrave Macmillan, Basingstoke, 2015), p. 197.
10. Jim Pickard, 'Exclusive: David Cameron and the Bullingdon night of the broken window', *Financial Times*, 4 April 2010.
11. Long and Burke, *Vandalism and Anti-Social Behaviour*, p. 197.
12. Nick Mutch, 'Bullingdon Club: behind Oxford University's elite society', *The Week*, 16 September 2019.
13. Mutch, 'Bullingdon Club', *The Week*.
14. Sherwood, 'Sexism, vandalism and bullying'.
15. Pippa Crerar, 'The Boris in China diaries: What's Chinese for "polymorphous"? How the Mayor's jokes got lost in translation', *Evening Standard*, 14 October 2013.
16. Purnell, *Just Boris*, p. 64.
17. Dower, *When Boris Met Dave*.
18. Stephen Evans, '"Mother's Boy": David Cameron and Margaret Thatcher', *The British Journal of Politics and International Relations*, volume 12, issue 3, 2010.
19. David Cameron, 'David Cameron book: The truth about me, cannabis and Eton', *The Times*, 14 September 2019.
20. Morris, *Oxford*, p. 259.

5. The Children's Parliament

1. Walter, *The Oxford Union*, p. 12.
2. Fiona Graham, *Playing at Politics: An Ethnography of the Oxford Union* (Dunedin Academic Press, Edinburgh, 2005), p. 28.
3. Christopher Hollis, *The Oxford Union* (Evans Brothers, London, 1965), p. 231.
4. Edward Heath, *The Course of My Life: My Autobiography* (A&C Black, London, 2011), retrieved through Google Books.
5. Benn Sheridan, 'An interview with Armando Iannucci', *Cherwell*, 4 June 2017.
6. Graham, *Playing at Politics*, p. 26.
7. Walter, *The Oxford Union*, pp. 22–3.
8. Morris, *The Oxford Book of Oxford*, p. 189.
9. Walter, *The Oxford Union*, pp. 12, 15, 33 and 46.
10. Walter, *The Oxford Union*, pp. 29, 117 and 191.
11. Graham, *Playing at Politics*, p. 70.
12. Louis MacNeice, 'Autumn Journal' (1939), retrieved at https://archive.org/stream/in.ernet. dli.2015.184237/2015.184237.Autumn-Journal_djvu.txt
13. Heath, *The Course of My Life*.
14. Walter, *The Oxford Union*, p. 69.
15. Christopher Hitchens, *Hitch-22* (Atlantic Books, London, 2011), p. 98.
16. Graham, *Playing at Politics*, p. 33.
17. Graham, *Playing at Politics*, p. 16.
18. Slates and backstabbing are well-described in Graham's *Playing at Politics*.
19. Graham, *Playing at Politics*, p. 206.
20. Dower, *When Boris Met Dave*.
21. Walter, *The Oxford Union*, p. 53.

6. The Bounder Speaks

1. Waugh, *Brideshead Revisited*, p. 255.
2. Graham, *Playing at Politics*, p. 182.
3. Dower, *When Boris Met Dave*.

Notes

4. John Evelyn, 'The Happy Couple', *Cherwell*, 8 February 1985.
5. Tina Brown, *The Vanity Fair Diaries: 1983–1992* (Henry Holt and Company, New York, 2017), retrieved through Google Books.
6. Toby Young, 'Cometh the hour, cometh the man: A profile of Boris Johnson', Quillette.com, 23 July 2019.
7. Dower, *When Boris Met Dave*.
8. Young, *When Boris Met Dave*, *Observer*.
9. Jane Mulkerrins, 'Frank Luntz: The man who came up with "climate change" – and claims to regret it', *The Times*, 25 May 2021.
10. Anthony Luzzato Gardner, *Stars with Stripes: The Essential Partnership between the European Union and the United States* (Palgrave Macmillan, London, 2020), p. 65.
11. Anne Applebaum, *Twilight of Democracy: The Seductive Lure of Authoritarianism* (Doubleday, New York, 2020), pp. 63–4.
12. Max Long, 'Boris Johnson calls for Thatcher College, Oxford,' *Cherwell*, 30 May 2013.
13. Simon Murphy, '"Meritocrat versus toff": Boris Johnson's losing battle for the Oxford Union', *Guardian*, 16 July, 2019.
14. Adonis, 'Boris Johnson', *Prospect*.
15. Evans, 'Norman Stone obituary', *Guardian*.
16. Kate Nicholson, 'Nick Robinson tells Boris Johnson to "stop talking" in awkward Radio 4 Interview', *Huffington Post*, 5 October 2021.
17. Purnell, *Just Boris*, p. 73.
18. John Evelyn, 'Action Man', *Cherwell*, 15 November 1985.
19. Mulkerrins, 'Frank Luntz', *The Times*.
20. Gimson, *Boris*, p. 70.
21. Purnell, *Just Boris*, p. 84.
22. Toby Young, 'Success and the also-rans', *Debate*, Michaelmas term, 1985.
23. Kenny, *Brief Encounters*.
24. Boris Johnson, 'Politics', in Johnson, *The Oxford Myth*, pp. 65–84.

7. Stooges, Votaries and Victims

1. Rob Merrick, 'Tories won't start wearing masks in Commons because they "know each other", Jacob Rees-Mogg says', *Independent*, 21 October 2021.
2. John Evelyn, 'Who Thinks They're Who', *Cherwell*, 15 November 1985.
3. John Evelyn, 'Gruesome Twosome II', *Cherwell*, 15 November 1985.
4. Owen Bennett, *Michael Gove: A Man in a Hurry* (Biteback Publishing, London, 2019), pp. 23 and 39.
5. Bennett, *Michael Gove*, pp. 28 and 31.
6. Tim Jotischky, 'Union debates sexual freedom', *Cherwell*, 17 October 1986.
7. Steve Bird, 'How the future PM, Boris Johnson, and NHS boss, Simon Stevens, formed an unlikely bond at Oxford', *Daily Telegraph*, 7 August 2019.
8. Gimson, *Boris*, p. 70.
9. Unsigned, 'Union slave auction', *Cherwell*, 6 June 1987.
10. Michael Gove, 'Class-ism', *Debate*, Michaelmas term, 1987.
11. Gove, 'The President's Address'.
12. John Mulvey, 'State of the Union', *Cherwell*, 5 February 1988.
13. Charles Moore, *Margaret Thatcher: The Authorized Biography, Volume One: Not For Turning* (Penguin UK, London, 2013).
14. David Blair and Andrew Page (ed.), *The History of the Oxford University Conservative Association* (OUCA, Oxford, 1995), pp. 15–16.
15. Johnson, 'Politics', in Johnson, *The Oxford Myth*, p. 72.
16. Julian Grenier, 'Fears for Conservative club', *Cherwell*, 16 October 1987.
17. Blair and Page (ed.), *The History of the Oxford University Conservative Association*, p. 39.
18. John Evelyn, 'Ego Bulge', *Cherwell*, 29 May 1987.
19. Jeremy Hunt, 'Moonie', *Cherwell*, 30 October 1987.
20. Robert Unsworth, 'Tories stripped of University title', *Cherwell*, 21 April 1989; Unsigned, 'You're Sick', *Cherwell*,

27 January 1989; and Unsigned, 'Cherwell Retrospective', *Cherwell*, 24 November 1989.

21. Julian Critchley, *A Bag of Boiled Sweets: An Autobiography* (Faber and Faber, London, 1994), pp. 49–50.
22. Walter, *The Oxford Union*, p. 141.
23. Jacob Rees-Mogg, 'It's the argument that counts, not the jolly old accent', *Sunday Times*, 23 May 1999.
24. Andy McSmith, 'Vote for Oxford!', *Independent*, 23 January 2010.
25. Michael Ashcroft, *Jacob's Ladder: The Unauthorised Biography of Jacob Rees-Mogg* (Biteback, London, 2019), retrieved through Google Books.
26. George Orwell, 'Boys' weeklies', published 1940, retrieved at https://www.orwell.ru/library/essays/boys/english/e_boys
27. Graham, *Playing at Politics*, p. 195.
28. John Evelyn, 'Barking', *Cherwell*, 11 January 1991.
29. Ehrenreich, *A Garden of Paper Flowers*, p. 198.
30. Anne Bradford and Richard Bradford, *Kingsley Amis* (Oxford University Press, Oxford, 1998), p. 1.
31. Jeremy Paxman, *The English: A Portrait of a People* (Penguin, London, 1998), pp. 189–90.

8. Union and Non-Union

1. Graham, *Playing at Politics*, p. 202.
2. Walter, *The Oxford Union*, p. 194.
3. Boris Johnson, 'Politics', in Rachel Johnson, *The Oxford Myth*, p. 65.
4. Graham, *Playing at Politics*, p. 30.
5. David Walter, *The Oxford Union: Playground of Power* (Macdonald, London, 1984), pp. 160–64.
6. Zoe Johnson, 'For a More Perfect Union', *Cherwell*, 20 November 1987.
7. Johnson, 'Politics', in Rachel Johnson, 'The Oxford Myth', p. 75.
8. Walter, *The Oxford Union*, p. 73.

9. Reg Little, 'A writer and a statesman', *Oxford Mail*, 22 May 2014.

10. Walter, *The Oxford Union*, p. 20.

11. Henry Hale, 'Labour ends Union boycott', *Cherwell*, 31 October 1986.

12. Hitchens, *Hitch-22*, p. 89.

13. Nigel Cawthorne, *Keir Starmer: A Life of Contrasts* (Gibson Square, London, 2021), p. 77.

14. Ed Balls, *Speaking Out: Lessons in Life and Politics* (Random House, London, 2016), retrieved through Google Books.

15. Cawthorne, *Keir Starmer*, p. 84.

16. Eleni Courea, 'How a young Boris Johnson bonded with NHS chief Simon Stevens', *The Times*, 6 August 2019.

17. Rowena Mason, 'Boris Johnson filmed telling Tory members NHS "needs reform"', *Guardian*, 25 June 2019.

18. Jo-Anne Pugh, 'Union may bar OUCA from next term', *Cherwell*, 24 October 1987.

9. Birth of Brexit

1. Valerie Grove, 'The Valerie Grove Interview: Patrick Robertson', *Sunday Times*, 16 June 1991.

2. Simon Heffer, 'The gadfly of Bruges', *Sunday Telegraph*, 14 April 1991.

3. Grove, 'The Valerie Grove Interview', *Sunday Times*.

4. John Evelyn, untitled, *Cherwell*, 17 February 1989.

5. Unsigned, 'The courtiers', *Evening Standard*, 21 November 1991.

6. Paul Vallely, 'A big little Englander', *Independent*, 25 April 1996.

7. John Evelyn, 'The Brat Pac', *Cherwell*, 10 February 1989.

8. Heffer, 'The gadfly of Bruges', *Sunday Telegraph*.

9. Cal McCrystal, 'Interview with Bruges Group founder member Patrick Robertson', *Independent on Sunday*, 16 June 1991.

10. William Cash, 'The deep history of Brexit', *Sunday Times*, 7 August 2016.

11. McCrystal, 'Interview with Bruges Group founder member Patrick Robertson', *Independent on Sunday*.

12. Philip Vander Elst, 'The EU Threat to Democracy and Liberty', The Bruges Group, 2015.

13. Heffer, 'The gadfly of Bruges', *Sunday Telegraph*.

14. Luke Harding and Harry Davies, 'Jonathan Aitken was paid £166,000 for book on Kazakh autocrat, leak suggests', 6 October 2021.

15. 'CV of Viktor Orbán', retrieved at http://2010-2015. miniszterelnok.hu/in_english_cv_of_viktor_orban/

16. Sam Knight, 'The man who brought you Brexit', *Guardian*, 29 September 2016.

17. Knight, 'The man who brought you Brexit', *Guardian*.

18. Knight, 'The man who brought you Brexit', *Guardian*.

19. https://twitter.com/IciLondres/status/1064944724241457153

20. Ashcroft, *Jacob's Ladder*, retrieved through Google Books.

21. John Evelyn, 'Enjoy', *Cherwell*, 12 June 1992.

22. Niels Bryan-Low, 'Oxford rejects Europe', *Cherwell*, 22 November 1991.

23. Ellis, *The Oxbridge Conspiracy*, p. 190.

24. Daniel Payne, 'In the LSE library archives – the founding of the Anti-Federalist League', LSE blogs, 26 September 2018.

25. Tim Shipman, *All Out War: The Full Story of Brexit* (William Collins, London, 2017), p. 25.

26. Vallely, 'A big Little Englander', *Independent*.

27. Gabriel Pogrund and Tim Shipman, 'May's Brexit chief was "student Sir Humphrey" bent on federal EU', *Sunday Times*, 11 February 2018.

28. Tom Peck, 'A chemist's son with the right formula for leadership', *Independent*, 6 October 2020.

29. Knight, 'The man who brought you Brexit'.

10. A Generation without Tragedy

1. Richard Colls, *This Sporting Life: Sport and Liberty in England, 1760–1960* (Oxford University Press, Oxford, 2020), pp. 227–9.
2. Wilson, *The Victorians*, p. 179.
3. Goodhart, *Head Hand Heart*, pp. 35–6.
4. Margaret Macmillan, *Peacemakers: Six Months That Changed the World* (John Murray, London, 2001), p. 425.
5. Walter, *The Oxford Union*, p. 46.
6. Walter, *The Oxford Union*, p. 33.
7. Charles Williams, *Harold Macmillan* (Phoenix, London, 2012), ebook edition, Locations 733–9.
8. Graham, *Playing at Politics*, p. 30.
9. Simon Ball, 'Prime Ministers in the First World War', history. blog.gov.uk, 4 August 2014.
10. Richard Davenport-Hines, *An English Affair: Sex, Class and Power in the Age of Profumo* (William Collins, London, 2013), pp. 5–6.
11. Williams, *Harold Macmillan*, Location 890.
12. Walter, *The Oxford Union*, pp. 222–4.
13. Morris, *Oxford*, p. 252.
14. Colls, *This Sporting Life*, p. 231.
15. George Orwell, 'In Defence of P. G. Wodehouse', in *The Collected Essays, Journalism and Letters of George Orwell, volume 3, As I Please: 1943–1945* (Penguin Books, Harmondsworth, 1987), p. 399.
16. Morris, *The Oxford Book of Oxford*, p. 336.
17. Williams, *Harold Macmillan*, Locations 9409–14.
18. Walter, *The Oxford Union*, p. 33.
19. Ball, 'Prime Ministers in the First World War'.
20. Trevor Timpson, 'World War One: The great and the good who were spared', BBC News, 20 March 2014.
21. 'Foreign News: Sir Anthony Eden: The man who waited', *Time*, 11 April 1955.
22. Gaddis Smith, 'A Gentleman and a scapegoat', *New York Times*, 23 August 1987.

23. Ball, 'Prime Ministers in the First World War'.
24. Walter, *The Oxford Union*, pp. 226–7.
25. *Church Times*, 'Sir Edward Heath', 2 November 2006.
26. Henry Buckton, *Politicians at War* (Leo Cooper, Barnsley, 2003), p. 2.
27. UK Parliament, 'James Callaghan, Lord Callaghan of Cardiff', retrieved at https://www.parliament.uk/about/living-heritage/transformingsociety/private-lives/yourcountry/collections/collections-second-world-war/parliamentarians-and-people/james-callaghan/ on 16 April 2021.
28. Ferdinand Mount, *Cold Cream: My Early Life and Other Mistakes* (Bloomsbury, London, 2009), p. 79.
29. Retrieved at https://www.iwm.org.uk/memorials/item/memorial/31943
30. Verkaik, *Posh Boys*, p. 60.
31. Andrew Roth, 'Michael Heseltine', *Guardian*, 20 March 2001.
32. Buckton, *Politicians at War*, pp. 11 and 4.
33. Hitchens, *Hitch-22*, p. 106.
34. Walker, *The President We Deserve*, p. 65.
35. Martin Walker, *The President We Deserve: Bill Clinton: His Rise, Falls, and Comebacks* (Crown Publishers, New York, 1996), p. 67.
36. Alessandra Stanley, 'Most likely to succeed', *New York Times*, 22 November 1992.
37. Talbott email, 4 December 2020.
38. Walker, *The President We Deserve*, p. 62–4.

11. Adults Now

1. Sampson, *The Changing Anatomy of Britain*, p. 167.
2. Ehrenreich, *A Garden of Paper Flowers*, p. 233.
3. Rajeev Syal, 'Dominic Cummings calls for "weirdos and misfits" for No 10 jobs', *Guardian*, 2 January 2020.
4. Parker, 'Dominic Cummings has "done" Brexit', *Financial Times*.

5. Luke McGee, 'Fiona Hill is right, the British are still total snobs about accents', CNN, 22 November 2019.
6. The Rush Limbaugh Show, 'Fiona Hill undermines multiple Democrat premises', 21 November 2019.
7. John Scalzi, 'Straight white male: The lowest difficulty setting there is', *Whatever*, 15 May 2012.
8. *Isis* magazine, untitled, Michaelmas term, 1987.
9. Alan Hollinghurst, 'A Snob's Progress', *New York Review of Books*, 27 May 2021.
10. Adonis, 'Importance of Being Eton'.
11. Geraldine Bedell, 'The Smooth Operator – Douglas Hurd', *Independent on Sunday*, 29 May 1994.
12. Adonis, 'Importance of Being Eton'.
13. Robert Saunders, 'The Cameron Illusion', Mile End Institute, Queen Mary University of London, 27 June 2016.
14. Bennett, *Michael Gove*, p. 43.
15. Verkaik, *Posh Boys*, p. 275.
16. Gideon Rachman, 'Memories of Britain's new chancellor', *Financial Times*, 12 May 2010.
17. Bennett, *Michael Gove*, p. 42.
18. Shipman, *All Out War*, p. 25.
19. Purnell, *Just Boris*, p. 95.
20. Purnell, *Just Boris*, pp. 101–3.
21. Gimson, *Boris*, p. 73.
22. John Evelyn, 'Paris and bust', *Cherwell*, 26 May 1989.
23. Verkaik, *Posh Boys*, p. 145.
24. Ellis, *The Oxbridge Conspiracy*, p. 276.
25. Tim Arango, 'Murdoch's "Head of Content"', *New York Times*, 28 April 2008.

12. Our House

1. Walter, *The Oxford Union*, p. 112.
2. Applebaum, *Twilight of Democracy*, p. 63.
3. Buruma, *The Churchill Complex*, pp. 277–8.
4. 'Boris Johnson en Anne Widdecombe bij de Oxford Debating

Society in 1998', video retrieved at https://www.youtube.com/watch?v=oe1BCozNUcE

5. Purnell, *Just Boris*, p. 157.
6. 'Michael Heseltine speech to Tory conference 1994 – IT WASN'T BROWN'S. IT WAS BALLS', retrieved at https://www.youtube.com/watch?v=4NB3neSNfmg
7. George Parker and Sebastian Payne, 'Boris Johnson is poised to become prime minister. Is he up to the job?', *Financial Times*, 4 July 2019.
8. Helen Lewis, 'Maybe we don't need to move Parliament to Hull. But we do need to overhaul its alienating traditions', *New Statesman*, 6 March 2015.
9. Graham, *Playing at Politics*, p. 155.
10. Williams, *Harold Macmillan*, locations 1357–64.
11. Applebaum, *Twilight of Democracy*, p. 63.
12. Wood, 'Diary', *LRB*.
13. Greg Hurst, 'Boris Johnson, the new Buddha of suburbia', *The Times*, 25 March 2008.
14. Applebaum, *Twilight of Democracy*, p. 68.
15. George Parker and Helen Warrell, 'Gove takes aim at Cameron's Etonians', *Financial Times*, 14 March 2014.
16. George Parker, 'David Cameron: The verdict so far', *Financial Times*, 16 March 2012.
17. Joy Lo Dico, 'The Sikorski set', *Evening Standard*, 26 June 2014.
18. Sebastian Shakespeare, 'My friend Boris, the great pretender', *Daily Mail*, 20 July 2019.

13. No Fighting in this Establishment

1. David Barsamian, 'Interview with John Pilger', *The Progressive Magazine*, 16 July 2007.
2. Wilson, *The Victorians*, p. 274.
3. Anthony Powell, *The Kindly Ones*: Book 6 of *A Dance to the Music of Time* (University of Chicago Press, 2010), retrieved through Google Books.

4. Janan Ganesh, 'Generation Balls in UK politics already reeks of yesterday', *Financial Times*, 23 September 2016.

14. Brexit and the Oxford Union

1. George Orwell, 'Second Thoughts on James Burnham', *Polemic*, summer 1946, retrieved at https://orwell.ru/library/reviews/burnham/english/e_burnh.html
2. Joseph O'Leary, 'What was promised about the customs union before the referendum?', Fullfact.org, 26 October 2018.
3. Shipman, *All Out War*, pp. 155–6.
4. Tom Gillespie, 'Who is Dominic Cummings: A former PM branded him a "career psychopath" – here's what you need to know about Boris Johnson's top aide', Sky News, 15 November 2020.
5. Alex Andreou, 'Boris Johnson has decided chaos and self-destruction is a price worth paying – as long as he gets to be in charge', inews.co.uk, 7 January 2019.
6. Jon Henley and Dan Roberts, '11 Brexit promises the government quietly dropped', *Guardian*, 28 March 2018.
7. Verkaik, *Posh Boys*, p. 166.
8. Knight, 'The man who brought you Brexit'.
9. Rowena Mason, 'Boris Johnson on Brexit: "We can be like Canada"', *Guardian*, 11 March 2016.
10. Roland Philipps, *A Spy Named Orphan: The Enigma of Donald Maclean* (The Bodley Head, London, 2018), retrieved through Google Books.
11. Ralph Glasser, *Gorbals Boy at Oxford* (Pan Books, London, 1990), pp. 63–4.

15. May I Count on Your Vote?

1. Nicholas D. Kristof, 'Hacking a path to Downing Street', *Washington Post*, 14 August 1982.
2. Shipman, *All Out War*, pp. 534–5 and 541.
3. Rosa Prince, *Theresa May: The Enigmatic Prime Minister* (Biteback, London, 2017), pp. 38–43.

4. Mark Vernon, '*Brief Encounters: Notes from a Philosopher's Diary*, by Anthony Kenny', *Church Times*, 30 November 2018.
5. https://twitter.com/Dominic2306/status/1448029839571685383
6. Verkaik, *Posh Boys*, p. 148.
7. Chloe Chaplain, 'Wykehamist: What the public school jibe Jacob Rees-Mogg made to Oliver Letwin means', inews.co.uk, 28 March 2019.
8. Kevin Rawlinson, '"Sit up!" – Jacob Rees-Mogg under fire for slouching in Commons', *Guardian*, 3 September 2019.
9. Evening Standard, 'Channel 4 Brexit Debate: Jacob Rees-Mogg lays into Theresa May's Brexit deal saying "it does not do what she said"', 9 December 2018.
10. Wood, 'Diary', *LRB*.
11. Applebaum, *Twilight of Democracy*, pp. 84–5.
12. George Parker, Jim Pickard and Laura Hughes, 'Theresa May wins vote of confidence', *Financial Times*, 13 December 2018.
13. Rowena Mason, 'Javid: Johnson should not face another Oxford graduate in runoff', *Guardian*, 17 June 2019.
14. Rory Stewart, 'Politics Lite: No sacrifice, no substance, no success', *New York Times*, 10 March 2007.
15. The UK in a Changing Europe, 'Beer and Brexit with Rory Stewart MP', YouTube, 14 March 2019.

16. The Chumocracy Pandemic

1. Retrieved at https://twitter.com/BBCBreaking/status/1417515644749336576?s=20
2. Reuters, 'UK lockdown a week earlier could have halved COVID-19 death toll, scientist says', 10 June 2020.
3. Thomas Reilly, 'Parliamentary Health & Social Care Committee Report into the UK's Covid-19 Response', Globalpolicywatch.com, 14 October 2021.
4. Alain Tolhurst, 'Cummings says reform of "disaster zone" civil service was a condition for entering No. 10', *Civil Service World*, 18 March 2021.

5. Patrick Grafton-Green, '"Inept" government slammed as Covid PPE losses of £8.7 billion revealed', LBC, 1 February 2022.
6. Good Law Project, 'It's time for an end to cronyism', 1 November 2020.
7. Manveen Rana (host), 'Tracking and tracing the rise of Dido Harding', Stories of our times podcast, 25 August 2020.
8. Kate Ng, 'Tory MP blames "chaotic parents" for children going to school hungry', *Independent*, 28 October 2020.
9. Archie Bland, 'Daily Telegraph rebuked over Toby Young's Covid column', *Guardian*, 15 January 2021.
10. Robert Shrimsley, 'Rightwing sceptics helped deepen the UK's Covid crisis', *Financial Times*, 6 January 2021.
11. George Parker, Sebastian Payne, Tom Burgis, Kadhim Shubber, Jim Pickard and Jasmine Cameron-Chileshe, 'Inside Boris Johnson's money network', *Financial Times*, 30 July 2021.
12. Jacqui Wise, 'Covid-19: NHS Test and Trace made no difference to the pandemic, says report', *British Medical Journal*, 10 March 2021.
13. UK Parliament, 'The Fallen: Military strength and deaths in combat', undated.
14. Danny Dorling, 'Why has the UK's COVID death toll been so high? Inequality may have played a role', PreventionWeb, 4 March 2021.
15. Lex, 'Serco: UK test and trace scheme boosts outsourcer', *Financial Times*, 14 June 2021.
16. Mutch, Myers, Lusher and Owen, 'General Election 2015', *Independent*.
17. Gill Plimmer, 'Serco chief Rupert Soames receives £4.9m pay package', *Financial Times*, 10 March 2021.
18. Martin Shipton, '"Boris Johnson is boxed in, vulnerable … but he could pull it off": The new Prime Minister's former right-hand man', Wales Online, 27 July 2019.
19. David Morrison, 'Lies, half-truths and omissions on the road to war against Iraq', Opendemocracy.net, 28 October 2015.

17. What Is To Be Done?

1. Dominic Cummings, 'Times op-ed: What Is To Be Done? An answer to Dean Acheson's famous quip', Dominic Cummings's blog, 4 December 2014.
2. Brooke Masters, 'How Britain's private schools lost their grip on Oxbridge', *Financial Times*, 2 July 2021.
3. Snow, *Oxford Observed*, pp. 101–2.
4. Oxford University Development Office, 'Celebrating the impact of philanthropy: £3.3 billion raised through the Oxford Thinking Campaign', 14 October 2019.
5. Parker, Payne, Burgis, Shubber Pickard and Cameron-Chileshe, 'Inside Boris Johnson's money network', *Financial Times*.
6. Nadeem Badshah and Richard Adams, 'Oxford vice-chancellor "embarrassed" to have Michael Gove as alumnus', *Guardian*, 1 September 2021.
7. Verkaik, *Posh Boys*, pp. 322–3.
8. Cherwell News, 'Access denied: Oxford admits more Westminster pupils than black students', *Cherwell*, 23 May 2018.
9. Tara Sallis, 'More Union Presidents than BME people in cabinet', *Cherwell*, 19 January 2018.
10. Graham, *Playing at Politics*, p. 206.
11. Hill, *There Is Nothing For You Here*, p. 320.
12. Masters, 'How Britain's private schools lost their grip on Oxbridge', *Financial Times*; and Adonis, 'State schools and the quiet revolution at Oxbridge', *Prospect*.
13. Richard Brooks, '"Elite v plebs": The Oxford rivalries of boys who would never grow up to be men', *Guardian*, 26 September 2021.
14. Hill, *There Is Nothing For You Here*, p. 320.
15. Harry Mount, 'Bye bye, Buller', *Spectator*, 18 February 2017.
16. Lydia Willgress and Sam Dean, 'Bullingdon Club at Oxford University faces extinction because "nobody wants to join"', *Daily Telegraph*, 12 September 2016.

17. Tom Gould, 'Tories revolt As OUCA President pushes through Bullingdon Club ban', *Oxford Student*, 1 November 2018.

18. John Simpson Architects, 'Debating Chamber Eton College', undated, retrieved at http://www.johnsimpsonarchitects.com/pa/Eton-College-hm.html on 19 July 2021.

19. Luke Mintz, 'Meet William Rees-Mogg, the nephew of Jacob, trying to sell Conservatism to a new generation', *Daily Telegraph*, 26 July 2017.

20. Adonis, 'State schools and the quiet revolution at Oxbridge', *Prospect*.

21. Retrieved at https://twitter.com/cornelban73/status/1259759306221764609

22. Jamie Doward, 'Head likens criticism of private schools to antisemitic abuse', *Guardian*, 11 May 2019.

23. Phillip Inman, 'Social mobility in richest countries "has stalled since 1990s"', *Guardian*, 15 June 2018.

24. Maclean's, 'Canada is one of the most socially mobile countries in the world. Here's why', 14 August 2018.

25. Malcolm Gladwell, 'Getting In', *New Yorker*, 2 October 2005.

26. Ouest-France with AFP, 'L'ENA aura disparu dès le 1er janvier 2022', 11 April 2021.

ACKNOWLEDGEMENTS

Many thanks to everyone interviewed for the book.

Michael Crick deserves a special shout-out. After submitting to interview, he then opened his unmatched contacts book, helping me reach several of the main actors in this story. He also applied his famed fact-checking skills to proofreading the manuscript. Any remaining mistakes are entirely my fault.

Dan Dombey, Andrew Franklin, Adam Kuper, James McAuley and Calah Singleton read the manuscript too, and made very helpful suggestions. Thanks also to Andrew for believing in this book from the start, and to Gordon Wise for selling it so vigorously. Ellen Hendry and Pauline Harris did invaluable research in Oxford archives.

I also want to thank Charles Aldington, Anthony of Dunedin Academic Press, Carl Bromley, Penny Daniel, Anna Davies, Christian Davies, Fred Defossard, John Foot, Penny Gardiner, Jasper Gibson, Constantine Gonticas, Victoria Hostin, Howard Jacobs, Tim Leunig, Edward Luce, Marianne Macdonald, Rana Mitter, Rebecca Nicholson, Ilaria Regondi, Alec Russell, Katrine Sawyer, Derek Shearer, Simon Skinner, Charlotte Thorne, Emma Tucker, Catherine de Vries, William Wright and Valentina Zanca.

This book grew out of an article I published in the *Financial Times* in 2019, and without my colleagues at the paper the whole thing would never have happened. Esther Bintliff, Piero Bohoslawec, Emma Bowkett, Andrea Crisp, Alice Fishburn, Sophie Hanscombe, Jane Lamacraft, Anthony Lavelle, Josh Lustig, Neil

O'Sullivan, Cherish Rufus, Alec Russell, Josh Spero and Matt Vella commissioned, edited, corrected, published and found photographs for several articles of mine that went into this book. I will always be grateful for their professionalism, political tolerance and devotion to accuracy. I'm also grateful to the *FT* for allowing me to reuse the material.

Pamela Druckerman puts up with me, so far, though I'm not sure why. She has all my love. So do Leila, Leo and Joey.

SELECT BIBLIOGRAPHY

Anne Applebaum, *Twilight of Democracy: The Seductive Lure of Authoritarianism* (Doubleday, New York, 2020)

Owen Bennett, *Michael Gove: A Man in a Hurry* (Biteback Publishing, London, 2019)

David Blair and Andrew Page (ed.), *The History of the Oxford University Conservative Association* (OUCA, Oxford, 1995)

Henry Buckton, *Politicians at War* (Leo Cooper, Barnsley, 2003)

Richard Colls, *This Sporting Life: Sport and Liberty in England, 1760–1960* (Oxford University Press, Oxford, 2020)

Julian Critchley, *A Bag of Boiled Sweets: An Autobiography* (Faber and Faber, London, 1994)

Rosa Ehrenreich, *A Garden of Paper Flowers: An American at Oxford* (Picador, London, 1994)

Walter Ellis, *The Oxbridge Conspiracy* (Penguin, London, 1995)

Andrew Gimson, *Boris: The Rise of Boris Johnson* (Simon & Schuster, London, 2006)

David Goodhart, *Head Hand Heart: The Struggle for Dignity and Status in the 21st Century* (Allen Lane, London, 2020)

Fiona Graham, *Playing at Politics: An ethnography of the Oxford Union* (Dunedin Academic Press, Edinburgh, 2005)

Francis Green and David Kynaston, *Engines of Privilege: Britain's Private School Problem* (Bloomsbury, London, 2019)

Christopher Hitchens, *Hitch-22* (Atlantic Books, London, 2011)

Dafydd Jones, *Oxford: The Last Hurrah* (ACC Art Books, Woodbridge, 2020)

Rachel Johnson (ed.), *The Oxford Myth* (Weidenfeld & Nicholson, London, 1988)

Jan Morris, *Oxford* (Oxford University Press, Oxford, 1987)

Jan Morris (ed.), *The Oxford Book of Oxford* (Oxford University Press, Oxford, 1979)

Rosa Prince, *Theresa May: The Enigmatic Prime Minister* (Biteback, London, 2017)

Sonia Purnell, *Just Boris: The Irresistible Rise of a Political Celebrity* (Aurum, London, 2011)

Anthony Sampson, *The Changing Anatomy of Britain* (Coronet Books, London, 1982)

Tim Shipman, *All Out War: The Full Story of Brexit* (William Collins, London, 2017)

Peter Snow, *Oxford Observed: Town and Gown* (John Murray, London, 1992)

Robert Verkaik, *Posh Boys: How the English Public Schools Run Britain* (Oneworld, London, 2018)

Martin Walker, *The President We Deserve: Bill Clinton: His Rise, Falls, and Comebacks* (Crown Publishers, New York, 1996)

David Walter, *The Oxford Union: Playground of Power* (Macdonald, London, 1984)

Evelyn Waugh, *Brideshead Revisited* (Penguin Classics, London, 2000)

A. N. Wilson, *The Victorians* (Arrow Books, London, 2003)

Films and TV

John Dower (director), *When Boris met Dave*, docudrama, 2009.

INDEX

Index

Index

Sumner, Humphrey 120
Sunak, Rishi 40, 115, 180

T
Talbott, Strobe 124–5
Tebbit, Norman 110
Thatcher, Margaret 3, 12, 27–8,
  30, 54, 55, 122, 133, 143–4, 153,
  175
  Bruges Group presidency
    (1991–2013) 112
  Europe, views on 99–100,
    101
  Farage and 112
  Gove and 81, 82
  Johnson and 70, 72
  OUCA presidency (1946) 83
  Rees-Mogg and 87, 99
  resignation (1990) 104, 132
  Robertson and 101, 102, 112
  Stone and 43
Thomson, Robert 137
Tolkien, John Ronald Reuel
  33, 35
Toynbee, Philip 165
Trump, Donald 11
Truss, Elizabeth 'Liz' 40
Tucker, Emma 5
Turing, Alan 38
Turnbull, Malcolm 63–4, 131,
  152, 155, 158, 183

Twigg, Stephen 96

V
Veksner, Simon 66
Vindman, Alexander 130

W
Walker, Martin 125
Walpole, Robert 45
Walter, David 59, 86
Wang Anshun 54
Waugh, Evelyn
  Brideshead Revisited (1945)
    28, 30, 32, 38, 42, 46, 53, 65,
    67, 68, 123, 161
  Decline and Fall (1928) 51, 175
  Union election (1923) 62
Wilde, Oscar 81
Williams, Charles 120, 143
Wilson, Andrew Norman 24,
  152
Wilson, James Harold 3, 94
Wodehouse, Pelham Grenville
  48, 66, 67, 120, 123, 168, 173
Wood, James 46–8, 145, 171–2

Y
Young, Michael 9
Young, Toby 9, 22, 30, 51, 68,
  75–6, 134, 180

231